GMAT®

Integrated Reasoning & Essay

This guide covers the Integrated Reasoning section on the GMAT and Executive Assessment exams, as well as the Essay section on the GMAT. Master the IR question types and discover strategies for optimizing performance on the essay.

Acknowledgements

A great number of people were involved in the creation of the book you are holding.

Our Manhattan Prep resources are based on the continuing experiences of our instructors and students. The overall vision for this guide was developed by Whitney Garner and Stacey Koprince, who developed the strategies for each question type and wove them into a cohesive whole.

Stacey Koprince was the primary author and she was supported by a number of content experts. Whitney Garner and Emily Meredith Sledge served as a sounding board during the writing phase, developing and vetting ideas and editing new content. Mario Gambino managed production for the many complex images, with Derek Frankhouser and Israt Pasha lending their design expertise.

Matthew Callan coordinated the production work for this guide. Once the manuscript was done, Naomi Beesen and Ben Ku edited and Cheryl Duckler proofread the entire guide from start to finish. Carly Schnur designed the covers.

Retail ISBNs: 978-1-5062-1967-7, 978-1-5062-6253-6
Retail eISBN: 978-1-5062-4920-9
Course ISBN: 978-1-5062-4921-6
Course eISBN: 978-1-5062-4922-3

GMAT® Strategy Guides

GMAT All the Quant

GMAT All the Verbal

GMAT Integrated Reasoning & Essay

Strategy Guide Supplements

<u>Math</u>

GMAT Foundations of Math

GMAT Advanced Quant

<u>Verbal</u>

GMAT Foundations of Verbal

September 3, 2019

Dear Student,

Thank you for picking up a copy of *Integrated Reasoning & Essay*. I hope this book provides just the guidance you need to get the most out of your GMAT studies.

At Manhattan Prep, we continually aspire to provide the best instructors and resources possible. If you have any questions or feedback, please do not hesitate to contact us.

Email our Student Services team at gmat@manhattanprep.com or give us a shout at 212-721-7400 (or 800-576-4628 in the United States or Canada). We try to keep all our books free of errors, but if you think we've goofed, please visit manhattanprep.com/GMAT/errata.

Our Manhattan Prep Strategy Guides are based on the continuing experiences of both our instructors and our students. The primary author of the 7th Edition Integrated Reasoning & Essay guide was Stacey Koprince. Project management and design were led by Matthew Callan, Mario Gambino, and Helen Tan. I'd like to send particular thanks to instructors Whitney Garner, Ben Ku, and Emily Meredith Sledge for their content contributions.

Finally, we are indebted to all of the Manhattan Prep students who have given us excellent feedback over the years. This book wouldn't be half of what it is without their voice.

And now that you are one of our students too, please chime in! I look forward to hearing from you. Thanks again and best of luck preparing for the GMAT!

Sincerely,

Chris Ryan
Executive Director
Product Strategy

TABLE OF CONTENTS

The GMAT and the EA

The GMAT (Graduate Management Admission Test) and the EA (Executive Assessment) are computer-adaptive exams used for admission into graduate management education programs. MBA programs are more likely to use the GMAT, while the EA is most commonly used for EMBA programs (though both exams are used for both types of programs).

Both exams are made by GMAC (Graduate Management Admissions Council) and both test the same content via the same question types. The primary differences are in the scoring and the length of the exams.

Both exams have Quant, Verbal, and Integrated Reasoning (IR) sections; the GMAT also has an Essay section. The EA is 1.5 hours long, while the GMAT is about 3.5 hours long, including breaks.

Both exams provide individual scores for each section of the exam. The GMAT combines the Quant and Verbal section scores into one score, called the Total, on a 200–800 scale. The EA combines the IR, Quant, and Verbal section scores into a Total score on a 120–180 scale.

The IR section on the two exams is very similar, but time management strategies differ a bit. Where the two exams differ, this guide will specify what you need to know for the exam that you're planning to take.

The Executive Mindset

These exams are complex. They feel like academic tests—math, grammar, logical reasoning—but they're really not! At heart, these exams are a test of your executive reasoning skills.

Executive reasoning is the official term for your ability to make all kinds of decisions in the face of complex and changing information. It makes sense, then, that graduate management programs would want to test these skills. It's crucial for you to understand *how* they do so because that understanding will impact both how you study for the test and how you take the test.

You do need to know various math and grammar facts, rules, and concepts in order to do well on the exam—and this makes the GMAT and EA feel similar to tests that you took in school. There's one critical difference though: In school, your teachers tested you on material they expected you to know how to handle. Your teachers wouldn't put something on the test that they pretty much *expected* you to get wrong. That would be cruel!

Well, it would be cruel if the main point of the exam was to test your mastery of those facts, rules, and concepts. But that isn't the main point of the GMAT or the EA. These exams primarily measure your executive decision-making: when to invest your limited time and mental energy and when *not* to.

In other words, both the GMAT and the EA want to know how you make business decisions. And no good businessperson invests in every single opportunity placed in front of them, just because it's there. You'll invest in a majority of the problems presented to you, but you *will* say no to some—the ones that look too hard or seem like they'll take too long to solve. These are literally bad investments.

If you try to use a "school mindset" on the test, you'll keep trying to answer the current problem because you think that you're supposed to be able to do everything. You'll waste a bunch of time and then you'll have to rush on other questions in the section. As a result, you may miss questions that you actually do know how to answer and your score will be lower than it could have been.

Instead, use your "business mindset" to carry you through the exam. When the test finds your limit, acknowledge that! Call it a bad investment and let that problem go, ideally before you've spent very much time on it. Choose an answer—any answer—and move on.

As in the real world, you're going to have to decide what to do based upon incomplete information. At times, you'll decide to abandon a particular problem forever—knowing you can't come back to it even if you have extra time at the end. Practice being comfortable making decisions with that uncertainty.

(Note: The GMAT never lets you go back to any question that you've already answered. The EA allows you to go back within a limited subset of questions, but not all. You'll learn more about this in Chapter 8.)

Extend the business mindset to your studies as well. If there are certain topics that you really hate, don't study them in the first place. You're just going to bail (guess quickly and move on) when one of those "investment opportunities" comes up.

One caveat: You can't bail on huge swaths of content. For example, don't bail on all questions that test percents, fractions, and ratios, as these topics comprise a large portion of the IR section. You can, though, bail on a subset—perhaps you'll bail on fraction problems that require algebra, but choose to try fraction problems that contain real numbers.

Start orienting yourself around your business mindset today. You aren't going to do it all. You're going to choose the best opportunities for you, as you see them throughout the test. When you decide not to pursue a particular investment, you're going to say no as quickly as you can and forget about it—don't waste precious resources on a poor investment opportunity. Move on to the next opportunity, feeling good about making sound investment decisions about what to do and what *not* to do.

In short, embrace the executive mindset!

How to Use This Guide

In This Chapter

- The Essay

- Integrated Reasoning

In this chapter, you will learn how to get the most out of this guide and other resources you may use as you prepare for these two sections.

CHAPTER 1 How to Use This Guide

The *GMAT Integrated Reasoning & Essay Strategy Guide* will help you prepare for the Integrated Reasoning (IR) section of the GMAT and Executive Assessment (EA), as well as the Analytical Writing Assessment (AWA, or Essay) section of the GMAT.

The Essay

The Essay is the least important section of the GMAT (and it doesn't appear on the Executive Assessment at all). You will just need to get a "good enough" score, and approximately 80% of test-takers cross that threshold. You probably won't need to spend very much time to get yourself ready for this section.

Still, you'll want to have a mental template in place to make it as easy as possible to write the essay; this guide will show you how.

For many students, working through the essay material in this guide will be enough to get ready for the Essay section. If you have access to our GMAT Interact™ essay lesson, you can use this resource in addition to or instead of the essay chapter in this guide.

If you are struggling to compose complex sentences, Appendix A of this guide will teach you how to write more advanced sentences. You may also find it useful to study the Sentence Correction unit of Manhattan Prep's *GMAT All the Verbal* or *GMAT Foundations of Verbal* guides.

You can test your skills using GMAC's GMAT Write™ program, the same software scoring system used on the real exam. For a small fee, you'll get a score and feedback on two essays. You'll be able to revise the essays and submit them again to see whether your score improves. If you're in one of our study programs, check your program details; you might already have access to GMAT Write™ for free.

Integrated Reasoning

On the GMAT, the Integrated Reasoning (IR) score is more important than the Essay score but usually less important than the Quant or Verbal score. As a result, you will likely spend more time studying Quant and Verbal than IR.

On the Executive Assessment, though, the IR score is about as important as the Quant and Verbal scores, so you will likely spend a similar amount of time getting ready for all three sections.

On both exams, the IR section tests you on a mix of quantitative and verbal skills. The problems don't resemble the kinds of problems you're used to seeing on standardized tests—and this unnerves some people at first. But IR more closely resembles the kind of real-world analysis that you already do every day at work, so as you learn how to handle each problem type, you may find that you end up preferring the IR section to the others.

IR tosses a whole bunch of data at you and expects you to figure out what information you do or don't need in order to solve the problem—just as you have to do every day in real life. IR also requires integration of quant, logic, and comprehension all in one problem—again, just like real life.

In short, IR is going to feel messy, chaotic, imprecise—in that sense, it won't feel like a typical standardized test. But if you orient yourself toward the idea that this is a real-life type of problem, you'll be *expecting* that information overload and so you'll be in a better position to handle this section.

Chapter 3, "Introduction to Integrated Reasoning," will give you an overview of the timing, scoring, and structure of this section, including the four types of IR problems. This chapter also introduces the UPS process: Understand, Plan, Solve. You'll use this process to answer every IR problem on the test.

Chapters 4–7 cover the four problem types, one per chapter. We think it is best to study the four types in the order they appear in this book.

Chapter 8 summarizes the strategies for each problem type and for the overall IR section. It also addresses decision-making strategies for both the GMAT and the EA.

Appendix A discusses how to write more complex sentences for the Essay section on the GMAT. Finally, Appendix B summarizes some of the common math topics that are tested on the IR section. For full treatment of these and other quant topics, as well as strategies that will help you solve more efficiently, see Manhattan Prep's *GMAT All the Quant* guide.

If you are studying for the EA, incorporate IR equally with your Quant and Verbal studies. Study all three types every week.

If you are studying for the GMAT, you will likely concentrate on Quant and Verbal for the first few weeks. That's fine, but don't wait until the end of your studies to look at the IR section; spread out the work relatively evenly over time. Plan to study one IR question type every few weeks, depending on the total length of your studies.

As you finish each chapter in this guide, practice your skills using the practice problems found in Atlas, Manhattan Prep's online study center. If you purchase any official materials, such as the *GMAT Official Guide* or the *EA Official Practice Questions* from GMAC® (the makers of both exams), you'll have access to additional online Question Banks of real IR problems from past administrations of the official test.

Finally, make sure to include the IR section when taking practice computer-adaptive tests (CATs). A lot of people studying for the GMAT skip the IR and Essay sections because they know that these sections are less important overall on that exam, but it's critical to practice under official test conditions.

You're ready to dive into the book. Good luck and happy studying!

The Argument Essay

In This Chapter

In this chapter, you will learn how to write a GMAT essay that will get you a good enough score on the Analytical Writing Assessment (AWA) section of the exam. You'll also learn why you need only a good enough score, not a great score.

CHAPTER 2 **The Argument Essay**

The Analytical Writing Assessment (AWA) is also known as the Essay section. It appears either first or last on the GMAT, depending upon which section order you choose. (Note: The Executive Assessment does not have an Essay section.)

Schools just want to see a good enough essay score, so it won't take you long to get ready for this section.

What Is the Argument Essay?

This section of the GMAT consists of one 30-minute essay that you type into the computer. In this essay, you'll examine a flawed argument very similar to the flawed arguments you see on Critical Reasoning (CR) problems.

The schools want to ensure that you can write in English well enough to handle graduate-level academic coursework. This essay is the only thing that schools know that you wrote completely on your own, since you could have had help on your application essays. The Essay score provides admissions officers with a "fine" or "not fine" on your ability to communicate well in written English.

The scoring scale runs from 0 (lowest) to 6 (highest) in half-point increments. (The essay is separately scored—it does not factor into your GMAT Total score of 200–800.)

According to the *GMAT Official Guide*, a 6.0 essay "presents a cogent, well-articulated critique of the argument and demonstrates mastery of the elements of effective writing," though there may still be minor flaws. At the other end of the spectrum, *No score* (a 0) means you've left the essay blank, written something off topic or in a language other than English (including gibberish), or just recopied the topic.

You'll be assessed on three sets of skills:

1. *Logical analysis*: How well do you dissect and evaluate the argument?

2. *Persuasive writing*: How clearly and convincingly do you express your thoughts?

3. *Language usage*: grammar, syntax, variety of vocabulary

The Essay chapter in the *Official Guide* describes the essay task and provides a few useful example essays, as well as a list of possible essay topics and other useful material.

What Score Is Good Enough?

Here is the scoring scale for the AWA section, along with the GMAT's corresponding qualitative labels and the associated percentiles. (Note: Percentiles can change over time.)

AWA score	Label	Percentile
6.0	Outstanding	88
5.5		79
5.0	Strong	53
4.5		42
4.0	Adequate	17
3.5		11
3.0	Limited	4
2.5		3
2.0	Seriously Flawed	2
1.5		2
1.0	Fundamentally Deficient	1
0.5		1
0.0	No Score	0

As shown in the table, about half of all test-takers score a 5.0 or better. Most schools consider a 4.5 or better good enough, and even a 4.0 will probably be okay, as the GMAT calls this score *Adequate*.

A score of 3.5 or lower, though, may raise more serious concerns for the school. They will likely review the actual text of your essay in order to determine whether they think you can handle business-school-level communications.

So your goal is to score a 4.5 or higher on the essay. This gives you a little leeway to fall short (4.0) and still be okay.

Both a computer and a human grade your essay so, unlike your other scores, you won't receive your AWA score until a week or two after your test. You will receive your AWA score when you receive your official score report from GMAC®. If you score a 3.5 or lower, then you will need to consider whether to take the test again in order to raise this score.

If you score a 4.0 and the rest of your scores are good, don't retake the test just to lift your AWA score. If, though, you're going to retake the GMAT anyway, put in a little more time on your essay preparation to hit the 4.5 level.

If you are relatively confident that you'll score a 4.5 or higher, then you can do minimal preparation:

- Read the rest of this chapter and follow the instructions in "How to Prepare for the Essay."
  - Do the essay when taking practice computer-adaptive tests (CATs).
  - Possibly use GMAT Write™ (you'll learn what this is later in this chapter).

- Go in with a game plan. Know the process you want to follow.
- Write a decent amount. Longer essays generally score higher.

However, if you think you're at risk of a score below a 4.0, then you've got more work to do. To judge your risk, ask yourself these questions:

- *How much experience do you have writing academic English?*
  - Did you rarely write essays in English in school?
  - Were your grades in English classes low?
  - In your job, do you rarely write anything longer or more formal than short emails?

- *Is your command of written academic English weak?*

  If you're unsure, choose a long Reading Comprehension (RC) passage at random and read it with no time pressure, then consider these questions:
  - Are there many words that you didn't understand?
  - Did you fail to understand sentences when they got too long?
  - Did you take 10 minutes or more to finish the passage, only to find that you had little idea what it meant?
  - Did you frequently translate back into another language?

- *Is your command of spoken English weak?*
  - Do you struggle to keep up with a conversation among native English speakers?
  - Do you have a lot more trouble understanding English over the phone than in person?
  - Do you frequently strain to formulate new or complex ideas in English?

If you answered "yes" to several of these questions, work through this chapter carefully and follow up with Appendix A of this guide. You'll also need to do more practice with the essay outside of your practice tests.

The Physical Mechanics of Essay Writing

You will be typing your essay into a text box on the computer screen. You can enter as much text as you want, but you can only see about 10 lines at once.

The system feels like a clunky, old-fashioned word-processing program. You have just a few buttons with standard functions:

Button	Function	Keyboard shortcuts
Cut	Cuts text and puts it on a clipboard.	Ctrl-X or Alt-T
Copy	Copies text onto the clipboard.	Ctrl-C or Alt-C
Paste	Pastes text from the clipboard.	Ctrl-V or Alt-A
Undo	Undoes the last edit you made. You can undo your last 10 edits.	Ctrl-Z or Alt-U
Redo	Redoes something you just undid. You can redo the last 10 undone actions.	Ctrl-Y or Alt-R

Navigation keys on the keyboard act as you expect:

Arrow keys move the cursor up, down, left, or right.

Enter or *Return* inserts a paragraph break and moves you to a new line.

Page Up moves the cursor up one screen.

Page Down moves the cursor down one screen.

Backspace removes the character to the left of the cursor.

Delete removes the character to the right of the cursor.

Home moves the cursor to the beginning of the line.

End moves the cursor to the end of the line.

You will not have standard formatting options, such as <u>underline</u>, *italic*, or **bold**. Do not use any text-message substitutes, symbols, or abbreviations.

There is no tab or indent. To start a new paragraph, press *Enter* or *Return* a couple of times to insert a blank line between paragraphs. If you like to indent the beginning of paragraphs, hit the space bar a small, consistent number of times (say, five).

You will not have spelling or grammar check. You can make a few mistakes without impacting your score, but if you have so many mistakes that a reader would be distracted or possibly even unsure about your intended meaning, then your score will go down. Don't, though, get so caught up in being grammatically perfect that you write a much shorter essay than you're capable of writing in half an hour. Follow spelling and grammatical rules well enough to make your meaning clear, but keep writing.

What the Argument Essay Asks

The Argument Essay asks you to analyze an argument—something with a conclusion and premises. In fact, it will look very similar to the arguments you see in the Critical Reasoning (CR) section of the exam, and your CR tools will come in handy as you tackle the essay.

The argument that you need to analyze will contain a conclusion, or big claim, along with a few premises. Here's an invented, slightly extreme example:

> The country of Tarquinia has a much higher rate of traffic accidents per person than its neighbors, and in the vast majority of cases one or more drivers is found to be at fault in the courts. Therefore, Tarquinia should abolish driver-side seatbelts and airbags in all new cars and prohibit companies from developing other safety measures that protect the driver. These measures will eliminate traffic accidents in Tarquinia by motivating drivers to drive safely.

Here, the conclusion is that *these measures* (abolishing driver-side safety measures) *will eliminate traffic accidents in Tarquinia by motivating drivers to drive safely*. The premises are listed in the first sentence: the high rate of traffic accidents and the finding of driver fault. The second sentence describes the proposed measures and can be seen as part of the conclusion.

These are the official instructions for the essay:

> Discuss how well reasoned you find this argument. In your discussion, be sure to analyze the line of reasoning and the use of evidence in the argument. For example, you may need to consider what questionable assumptions underlie the thinking and what alternative explanations or counterexamples might weaken the conclusion. You can also discuss what sort of evidence would strengthen or refute the argument, what changes in the argument would make it more logically sound, and what, if anything, would help you better evaluate its conclusion.

Let's break these four sentences down. The first sentence is the most important:

Sentence 1:   *Discuss how well reasoned you find this argument.*

The argument will *never* be very well reasoned! Your goal is to find the flaws and explain them clearly.

Sentence 2:   *In your discussion, be sure to analyze the line of reasoning and the use of evidence in the argument.*

Line of reasoning:

- Does the conclusion follow completely logically from the premises? (It never does!) Why not?
- What and where are the gaps? Under what circumstances does the logic fail?
- What would help the author prove the conclusion?

Use of evidence:

- Does the evidence truly prove what the author wants it to? (It never does!) Why not?
- What does the given evidence actually prove? Under what circumstances?

Sentence 3:   *For example, you may need to consider what questionable assumptions underlie the thinking and what alternative explanations or counterexamples might weaken the conclusion.*

Questionable assumptions:

- At each stage of the logic, what has the author assumed that is not necessarily justified?

Alternative explanations or counterexamples:

- What else might explain the facts?
- What situations, cases, or circumstances has the author overlooked?

Sentence 4:   *You can also discuss what sort of evidence would strengthen or refute the argument, what changes in the argument would make it more logically sound, and what, if anything, would help you better evaluate its conclusion.*

The items listed in the fourth sentence are worthwhile but *less* important. You can get a 6.0 without including any of these aspects.

You are not asked to argue *for* or *against* the conclusion. Don't say whether you agree or disagree with it. Rather, pretend a friend has asked you to check his argument before he presents it to his boss. Help him analyze the logical strength of his argument: how well the conclusion is supported by the premises.

How to Manage Your Time

To write a decent essay in only 30 minutes, you'll need a clear process, such as the 5-step one below:

1. Read (1–2 minutes)
2. Brainstorm (2 minutes)
3. Outline (1–2 minutes)
4. Write (20 minutes)
5. Polish—a little (3–5 minutes)

Here's a short description of each step. You'll learn more about steps 2, 3, and 4 later in this chapter.

Step 1: Read (1–2 minutes)

First, clear your mind and read the argument slowly and carefully. Don't race through the reading. Thirty minutes is not very long, but if you don't take time to understand the argument, you won't write a very good essay.

As you read, identify the conclusion—the big claim that the author is making. The rest of the argument typically consists of background information and premises—facts and smaller claims made to support the conclusion. This support will always be flawed in some way, and those flaws will be based on gaps between the premises and the conclusion. Your job is to find those gaps.

Step 2: Brainstorm (2 minutes)

Some flaws will jump right out at you; others may take some thought. Jot down your ideas on your scratch paper or type them directly into the computer. Either way, don't write too much at this point—just enough to remind you of your thoughts.

Step 3: Outline (1–2 minutes)

Type a short placeholder into the text box for each paragraph, including an introduction, some body paragraphs, and a conclusion.

Step 4: Write (20 minutes)

Now, start writing. The three scored examples in the *Official Guide* show a clear pattern:

Score	Word count
6.0	335
4.0	260
2.0	108

The higher-scoring essays do tend to have more words. Aim for around 300 words.

Conveying complex information typically requires complex sentences. In fact, higher-scoring test-takers typically write longer sentences than lower-scoring ones, as noted in the table below:

Score	Word count	Sentences	Words per sentence
6.0	335	13	25.8
4.0	260	15	17.3
2.0	108	8	13.5

Train yourself to write approximately 20 words a sentence, not as a strict measure to apply in every case, but rather as a rough average. If you write 15 sentences averaging 20 words per sentence, you'll have 300 words (though one very short sentence can really stand out when you have an important point to make). Later in this chapter, you'll learn more about how to write better GMAT sentences.

Step 5: Polish—a little (3–5 minutes)

With a few minutes to go, turn off the spigot. Glance back over what you've written and smooth out the worst of the rough edges. Make sure you've removed any leftover text from your brainstorm or outline. Don't take too much time on any one sentence, gnawing your pen to find the *mot juste* (the "perfect word" in French); you only need a *good enough* score on the essay. Don't try to be Shakespeare.

When you're done, the test asks you to click next and submit, as on all sections. If you run out of time before you get to this, everything you've written will still be submitted.

If you're doing test order one, for which the essay is the first section, and you finish early, you may want to sit and let the timer run out. Use the extra time to close your eyes or gaze up at the wall, roll your shoulders around, and stretch in your seat.

How to Generate Good Ideas

As mentioned earlier, you'll need to brainstorm several flaws from the argument.

The key to brainstorming is to follow a method, four of which are described below. Try them out and use the method that works best for you.

Whichever method you use, jot down just enough to capture the idea; you don't have much time. Then, look for another idea. Here's how: Imagine that the flaw that you just spotted is now fixed. What *else* is wrong with the argument? Once you've identified three flaws, move to the outline phase.

Brainstorming Method 1: Line by Line

Start with the first sentence in the argument. What's wrong with it?

- If it's a piece of evidence, how does it fall short in proving the bigger point?
- If it's a claim, how is it not supported by the evidence?

Work your way, sentence by sentence, to the end of the argument.

Brainstorming Method 2: The CAST System

CAST is an acronym to remind you what you're looking for:

Counterexamples

- What situations would disprove the author's assertions?

Assumptions

- What is the author assuming, probably in an unjustified way?

Strengthen

- What would strengthen the argument?

Terms

- What specific words or terms in the argument create logical gaps or other problems?

Go letter by letter through CAST and jot down ideas.

Brainstorming Method 3: Use the Instructions

You'll always be provided with the same instructions, so you can use them as a checklist. The first sentence gives you the core task. The second sentence reminds you what to look *at*:

- Line of reasoning
- Use of evidence

The third sentence reminds you what to look *for*:

- Questionable assumptions
- Alternative explanations or counterexamples

Finally, the fourth sentence reminds you about other stuff you can add to your essay.

Brainstorming Method 4: Remember Common Fallacies

In the sample essay prompts (and in Critical Reasoning arguments), many of the same logical fallacies show up again and again. If you have trouble spotting flaws, here are some common ones to look for:

1. **Alternative Causes**

    If the author asserts that X causes Y, what *else* could be the cause of Y?

    Correlation ≠ Causation: If X and Y happen at the same time, it's not necessarily true that X causes Y. It could be that Y causes X, or some Z causes them both, or they just randomly happened together on this one occasion.

    After ≠ Because: If Y happens *after* X, it's not necessarily true that Y happens *because of* X. Some other cause could be at work.

    Future ≠ Past: If X did cause Y in the past, will X always cause Y in the future? Not necessarily. Circumstances could change.

2. **Unforeseen Consequences**

   If the author proposes plan A to achieve goal B, what could go *wrong*?

   Nothing's Perfect: How could the plan fail to achieve the stated goal? Does it go too far or not far enough? What implementation challenges has the author overlooked?

   Isn't It Ironic: What bad side effects of the plan could happen? These side effects might be bad on their own or they might directly prevent the plan from achieving its goal. Economic examples of the latter include customer attrition (e.g., if you raise prices to increase revenue, customers may flee) and price wars (e.g., if you cut your price to gain market share, your competition could cut prices in response). Think about who has been ignored by the author (such as customers and competitors) and what their negative responses to the plan might be.

   Skill & Will: If people are involved in implementing the plan (and they always are), you need the people to have both the *skill* to succeed and the *will* to succeed. Do they? Who benefits from the plan and are they the same people who need to carry it out?

3. **Faulty Use of Evidence**

   What is sketchy about the evidence?

   Limited Sample: Do you have too little data? How are the mentioned cases not representative of the wider world?

   Troubled Analogy: If the author draws a conclusion about M from facts about "similar" N, how are M and N different? What differing conditions has the author ignored?

   What It Really Means: The evidence simply may not imply what the author claims that it does.

4. **Faulty Use of Language**

   What ***extreme*** words does the author use? What ***vague*** terms are in the argument? You may even encounter a math fallacy, such as an argument that makes assumptions about real quantities when only percents have been given.

Now that you have plenty of ideas about possible flaws (and how to brainstorm them), look at the flaws described in an example essay: the 6.0 essay in the *Official Guide*. The given argument proposes an automatic early warning system to eliminate midair collisions between airplanes. Four flaws in this argument are pointed out in the second paragraph of the essay. Here's a brief list, as if they were brainstormed:

- Assumes cause of collisions = lack of knowledge
  - What if pilots don't pay attention to the warning system?
- Assumes pilots automatically obey the warning
  - What if they don't?
- Limited to commercial planes
  - What about other kinds of planes?
- What if the system fails?

The first two flaws are examples of the *Skill & Will* fallacy. The last two flaws are examples of *Nothing's Perfect*: The plan doesn't go far enough, and it ignores the possibility of failure.

Not every flaw in the argument is captured in the essay. That's fine! For instance, the author never criticizes the use of the extreme word *eliminate* in the conclusion (*reduce* would be more defensible). You do not need to address every last flaw in the argument.

Go ahead and brainstorm flaws in the Tarquinia argument. Take a few minutes and use any method you prefer in order to generate several specific flaws. Here is the prompt again; cover up the answers below the box until you have finished brainstorming.

> The country of Tarquinia has a much higher rate of traffic accidents per person than its neighbors, and in the vast majority of cases one or more drivers is found to be at fault in the courts. Therefore, Tarquinia should abolish driver-side seatbelts and airbags in all new cars and prohibit companies from developing other safety measures that protect the driver. These measures will eliminate traffic accidents in Tarquinia by motivating drivers to drive safely.

Here are some examples of flaws in this argument:

Higher accident rate = meaningful? • What if Tarquinia is not comparable to its neighbors? (car ownership, rural/urban mix might be different)	*Troubled Analogy*
Guilt in courts = true guilt? • What if courts are bad or just bureaucratic? Ignores other factors.	*What It Really Means*
Bad assumption: Drivers have the capability to prevent all or most accidents. (Maybe it's always icy in Tarquinia.)	*Skill & Will*
Removing safety features applies only to new cars. • System only works if all drivers are driving the cars made less safe.	*Nothing's Perfect*
Who would buy new cars? No one!	*Isn't It Ironic*

On first reading the argument, you may have felt that the proposed measures were extreme or impractical. However, you aren't supposed to talk about whether *you* yourself agree with the plan.

Instead, imagine how other people and companies would react. It would be nearly impossible to get car manufacturers, dealers, and the rest of the population to stick to the plan.

How to Structure the Essay

A good GMAT essay has three parts:

1. Introduction
2. Body
3. Conclusion

How you structure the body can vary, but your introduction and conclusion will be structured fairly similarly regardless of the specific argument you're given.

Introduction

First, briefly restate the argument's main claim or conclusion; if the argument is a plan, state the plan. Do not simply quote the argument; put it into your own words to show that you understood it:

> The author proposes plan X to accomplish goal Y . . .

Next, introduce your thesis statement: The argument is fundamentally flawed in some serious way.

For example, the thesis of the 6.0 example essay in the *Official Guide* is as follows:

> *The argument . . . omits some important concerns that must be addressed to substantiate the argument.*

Notice how general this thesis is. The essay writer is saying in a fancy way that the argument doesn't work. Here are some other examples:

> This plan is fundamentally flawed, in that the evidence provided fails to support the author's claim.

> The author makes several assumptions that are unlikely to be true, in which case her argument is seriously compromised.

To bulk up the intro paragraph, mention one or two of the most egregious flaws you discovered. Don't go into detail; you'll do that in the body of the essay.

If you'd like to give a positive nod to the argument, do so *before* your thesis, using a concession word such as *although*:

> Although the argument has some merits, a number of defects undermine the claim that . . .

Body

Describe and justify three to four specific flaws from the argument. If you brainstormed more than four flaws, pick the best and drop the rest. There are several ways to structure your body paragraph(s) to describe these flaws.

You can put all the flaws in one big paragraph, as the 6.0 example essay in the *Official Guide* does.

You can also describe each flaw in one sentence, then justify it in the next:

> The author fails to consider whether removing safety features in new cars will impact sales of new cars. If most potential customers decide to buy older used cars instead, then most cars will still have the safety features, derailing part of the author's plan.

> The author's evidence also falls short of establishing that drivers are actually capable of avoiding all accidents. Drivers are found to be at fault in "the vast majority" of cases, not all of them. In addition, even when someone is found to be at fault legally, it is not necessarily the case that she or he could have prevented the accident by driving more carefully.

In this case, save your discussion of improvements for the conclusion.

Alternatively, you can put each flaw in a separate body paragraph. Introduce the flaw, justify it, and then discuss how the author could address the flaw. For example:

> The author's evidence falls short of establishing that drivers are actually capable of avoiding all accidents. Drivers are found to be at fault in "the vast majority" of cases, not all of them. At least some drivers, then, could be seriously injured or even killed through no fault of their own, surely not the intended consequence of this law. In addition, the author appears to fail to realize that the safety features would be absent in both cars, so both the driver who caused the accident and the one who is the victim will be hurt or killed! Under those circumstances, the author may well achieve his stated goal, because it is unlikely that anyone will ever drive again.

You can even group a couple of flaws together in one paragraph, if they are related. For example, you could make one body paragraph about *poor use of evidence* (with two to three flaws) and another about *faulty line of reasoning* (with another two to three flaws).

Conclusion

1. Restate briefly *that* the argument is flawed and recap *why* this is the case:

   In summary . . .

2. Mention potential fixes to the line of reasoning used in the argument, if you haven't already:

   To address the problems in the argument, one would have to . . . (gather more data of XYZ kind) (run pilot projects to test the hypothesis) (etc.).

Use new language in your recap. You're saying, yet again, that the argument is flawed, but you need a novel way to say it. Replace particular words (e.g., flaw) with synonyms (error, gap, mistake, defect, fault, imperfection).

If you haven't already discussed possible improvements, do so here. If you are searching for still other things to say—and you have time—revisit the last sentence of the instructions. You can discuss possible new evidence or ways to evaluate the argument. Note that the 6.0 essay published in the *Official Guide* only briefly mentions potential improvements, so it's not necessary to do this. All that essay really does is explain the flaws; only the very last sentence gives a nod to fixes.

By the way, avoid humor in general; it can be easily misinterpreted in print. However, don't be afraid to let your personality shine through, if that helps you generate the volume of content you need.

Sample Essay

Had enough sentence analysis? Itching to get on with it and *write*?

Here's the Tarquinia essay again. On your computer, open up a basic word processor (WordPad or NotePad), one that doesn't have a spelling or grammar check. Alternatively, open up Microsoft Word (or a Google Doc) and disable automatic spelling/grammar check.

Set a timer for 30 minutes and write your essay.

The country of Tarquinia has a much higher rate of traffic accidents per person than its neighbors, and in the vast majority of cases one or more drivers is found to be at fault in the courts. Therefore, Tarquinia should abolish driver-side seatbelts and airbags in all new cars and prohibit companies from developing other safety measures that protect the driver. These measures will eliminate traffic accidents in Tarquinia by motivating drivers to drive safely.

Discuss how well reasoned you find this argument. In your discussion, be sure to analyze the line of reasoning and the use of evidence in the argument. For example, you may need to consider what questionable assumptions underlie the thinking and what alternative explanations or counterexamples might weaken the conclusion. You can also discuss what sort of evidence would strengthen or refute the argument, what changes in the argument would make it more logically sound, and what, if any- thing, would help you better evaluate its conclusion.

When you're done, cut and paste the results into Microsoft Word so that you can do a word count. Recall that you're aiming for approximately 300 words and about 15 sentences, for an average of 20 or so words per sentence. If your essay has substantially fewer than 300 words or an average of much less than 20 words per sentence, you'll need to bulk up.

Next, run the spelling and grammar check. Note any errors and figure out how you could fix them.

Now, take a look at a sample essay for the Tarquinia prompt. While this essay is not perfect, it would likely score a 5.5 or 6.0:

2

> In response to the comparatively high rate of traffic accidents in Tarquinia, the author argues that measures should be taken to compromise driver safety in order to motivate safer driving. This argument suffers from a number of flaws, ranging from flimsy use of evidence to ill-conceived elements of the proposal.
>
> First of all, the author cites two pieces of supporting evidence that, even if true, may not actually support the conclusion. Tarquinia may have a higher rate of accidents than its neighbors, but what if those neighbors have vastly different circumstances? Rates of car ownership, highway safety conditions (even including weather), and urban/rural divides could all contribute to the higher rate in Tarquinia. Likewise, it may be true that Tarquinian courts find one or more drivers at fault in most cases, but the degree to which these findings are driven by administrative necessity or other unrelated factors is unknown. Perhaps insurance law in the country demands that one or the other driver be found at fault, even if road conditions are largely to blame.
>
> Secondly, the design of the plan appears to be unworkable, even without consideration of the moral implications; for example, some accidents are the result of factors outside of anyone's control. Moreover, the fact that the proposal only applies to new cars creates another logical hole big enough to drive a truck through. Most car buyers would not willingly purchase a new car, and if anyone did, the presence of old cars (which would still have the old safety measures) would undermine the plan, since not all drivers would be subject to the same risk of harm for poor driving.
>
> In order to improve the proposal, the author would need to establish, first, that removing safety features would actually cause drivers to change their behavior and drive much more carefully. Second, the author would need to modify the plan such that all drivers were driving under the same conditions—perhaps older models would have their safety features removed. Even then, the fact that weather or road conditions will inevitably still cause some accidents renders this plan morally suspect.

Compare how you expressed a point with how the essay above expressed a similar point. Borrow or steal whatever you find useful—word choices, phrasing, sentence or paragraph structure. How can you do that? Retype the phrases or sentences you want to steal, making any tweaks you like to fit your writing style.

How to Vary Sentence Structure and Content

How could you improve this sample paragraph?

> The safety features are one major flaw in the argument. Safety features will only be removed from new cars. Only some drivers will have such a strong incentive to avoid all accidents. Some people may even avoid buying new cars. Removing the safety features may not be the deterrent that the author hopes.

The paragraph contains some good ideas, but the presentation of those ideas could be better. The sentences are pretty short, and three of the five use *safety features* as the subject. The ideas aren't very well connected to each other, and the last sentence could use a transition word to indicate more clearly that it is summarizing the paragraph.

Take a look at this example:

> The author fails to consider the potential ramifications of removing the safety features. The removal will take place only for new cars, so only a subset of drivers will have a very strong incentive to avoid all accidents, creating an imbalance among different drivers on the road. Some may counter that this drawback will disappear as more people buy new cars, but the safety feature mandate may actually cause people to prefer used cars to new ones, perpetuating the imbalance long-term. In short, removing the safety features from new cars may not be the deterrent that the author hopes.

In the second example, the author combines some sentences in order to better connect the ideas and varies the structure so that the subjects aren't always the same. The author also adds modifiers (e.g., *creating an imbalance...road*) to increase the complexity of the discussion and add nuance. Finally, the author uses a transition phrase, *in short*, to indicate that the last sentence summarizes the main point of the paragraph.

As you write, keep three aspects in mind:

1. A sentence should contain one clear, central thought.

2. Use modifiers to add complexity and nuance to the main thought.

3. Use signal words, such as *therefore*, *however*, and *in short*, to signal transitions to the reader.

For more, read Appendix A: "How to Write Better Sentences" at the end of this book.

An Analysis of the Sample Essay

Let's examine each sentence in the sample essay from earlier in this chapter.

Paragraph 1, Sentence 1:

In response to X...	*the author*	*argues*	*that*	*measures*	*should be taken to Y.*
Opening Modifier	Subject	Verb	THAT	Subject	Verb

The writer is summarizing the claim made by the author of the argument. This could have been spread across two sentences, but the writer collapses them into one through use of an opening modifier, a very effective way to write a more complex sentence.

Paragraph 1, Sentence 2:

This argument	*suffers*	*from a number of flaws*	*, ranging from A to B.*
Subject	Verb	Prepositional Phrase	Modifier

The writer then asserts a thesis—that the argument is flawed—and explains two parallel reasons why (A and B). The reader would expect later discussion in the essay to provide examples of these two reasons why.

Again the author adds a modifier to extend the sentence rather than write two separate sentences. This time, the modifier is at the end.

Paragraph 2, Sentence 1:

The author	*cites*	*evidence*	*that . . . may not . . . support the conclusion.*
Subject	Verb	Object	Modifier

Are you noticing a trend? Modifiers are an excellent mechanism for writing a more complex sentence. The first sentence of the essay had an opening modifier and the second used a comma *–ing* modifier. This third one uses a noun modifier that provides additional information about the *evidence* cited by the author.

Paragraph 2, Sentence 2:

Tarquinia may have a higher rate of accidents . . .	*, but*	*what if those neighbors have vastly different circumstances?*
Complete Sentence	, Conjunction	Complete Sentence

You can also create a compound sentence: two independent clauses, or complete sentences, connected by a comma and conjunction.

Also, asking a question can be an effective way to get the reader to consider a particular flaw in the logic.

Paragraph 2, Sentence 3:

Rates of ownership,	*highway conditions,*	*and*	*urban/rural divides . . .*
Subject	Subject	Conjunction	Subject

Parts of sentences can be compound in form as well. This sentence has a compound subject in the form of a list of three things.

Paragraph 2, Sentence 4:

It may be true that . . .	*, but*	*the degree . . . is unknown.*
Complete Sentence	, Conjunction	Complete Sentence

This is another compound sentence with an intricate second half:

. . . the degree	*to which these findings are driven by administrative necessity or other unrelated factors*	*is unknown.*
Subject	Modifier	Predicate

The modifier is a mouthful. It's actually a bit difficult to understand. (What is *administrative necessity*?) Your essay doesn't need to be perfect. The test writers understand that this is an impromptu writing exercise; they're willing to overlook some flaws.

Paragraph 2, Sentence 5:

Perhaps the law demands that one or the other be found at fault,	*even if road conditions are to blame.*
Independent Clause	Dependent Clause

You're now encountering a sentence-level subordinate clause: [*main sentence*], *even if* [*subordinate clause*]. The second part cannot stand alone as written; it has to be attached to an independent clause.

This sentence also begins with the word *perhaps*, signaling that the writer is speculating. This is another effective way to illustrate potential weaknesses in an argument.

Paragraph 3, Sentence 1:

The design appears unworkable	*, even without X*	*;*	*for example, some accidents are the result of Y.*
Complete Sentence	Modifier	Semicolon	Complete Sentence

Two related sentences can be connected with a semicolon, but don't just toss in this device anywhere. There should be a good reason to connect two sentences in this way. The first part of the sentence makes a particular claim; the second half provides an example to illustrate that claim.

Paragraph 3, Sentence 2:

The fact	*that the proposal only applies to new cars*	*creates another hole.*
Subject	Modifier	Predicate

You can put a complex noun modifier in between the main subject and verb. In this case, the *that* modifier introduces a clause with its own subject and verb.

Paragraph 3, Sentence 3:

Most buyers would not purchase a car	*, and*	*if anyone did*	*, the presence of old cars would undermine the plan*	*, since not all drivers would be subject to the same risk.*
Complete Sentence	, Conjunction	Subordinate Clause	Complete Sentence	Subordinate Clause

This is a long one—more than 30 words! The sentence is a little unwieldy; the writer should probably have broken it into two sentences. Still, this is a legitimate compound sentence, and the second sentence does have two legitimate subordinate clauses attached to it. The test is not going to penalize you for having a few sentences that go on a bit long, as long as the sentence is still intelligible.

Paragraph 4, Sentence 1:

In order to . . .	*the author would need to establish*	*, first, that removing A would cause drivers to B and C.*
Opening Modifier	Complete Sentence	Modifier

The ending modifier has a pretty complex structure. First, it has a cause–effect setup: Removing one thing would cause another. Second, there are in fact two effects, presented in parallel form: *change their behavior* and *drive much more carefully.*

The sentence also foreshadows, through the use of the word *first*, that the author would need to do two things *in order to improve the proposal.* The second thing should come in the next sentence.

Paragraph 4, Sentence 2:

Second,	*the author would need to modify the plan*	*such that . . .*	*—perhaps . . .*
	Complete Sentence	Subordinate Clause	Complete Sentence

You can also add a second complete sentence by setting that sentence off with a couple of hyphens (--) or an em-dash (—). For the latter, the keyboard shortcut is CTRL-Alt-Minus (on the numeric keypad).

Paragraph 4, Sentence 3:

Even then,	*the fact*	*that conditions will cause accidents*	*renders this plan suspect.*
	Subject	Modifier	Predicate

In the first two sentences of this paragraph, the writer does offer some ways for the author of the argument to improve the argument but this final sentence signals that the writer thinks the proposal is fundamentally flawed even if such fixes were to be made. You don't necessarily need to say something like this; you may think that the argument you're given could be fixed if certain flaws were appropriately addressed.

How to Prepare for the Essay

Now that you've gotten this far, do a few more practice essays to get ready:

1. **Do the Argument Essay section on all of your practice CATs.**

   You have a built-in chance to practice your essay writing when you take a practice test. You also want to make sure you're taking tests under full testing conditions, since mental stamina is an issue over the nearly 3.5-hour length of the exam. When you're done, check the essay in the same way described in this chapter: Paste it into Microsoft Word to check word count, spelling, and grammar, then take the time to rewrite any problematic parts to solidify your learning for next time.

2.   **Do GMAT Write®.**

You may or may not need to take this step. GMAT Write is a service offered by the makers of the GMAT. You practice with real prompts and are scored by the same computer algorithm as that used on the real exam.

You can purchase access to GMAT Write on the mba.com website. If you are a Manhattan Prep student, check the details of your program, as it may already include this service.

If you score a 4.5 or higher on GMAT Write, you're good to go (though still practice your essay on practice tests). If your score comes back as a 3.5 or lower, see the next section of this chapter. Finally, if you get a 4.0, you're on the cusp. Put a bit more time into your essay prep just to make sure that you don't fall below a 4.0 on the real test.

Additional Preparation

If you have scored a 3.5 or lower on GMAT Write or on the real Essay section—or you think you will—you need to put more time into preparing for the essay.

Here are practical steps to take:

Step 1: Work Through Manhattan Prep's *GMAT Foundations of Verbal Strategy Guide*

You may already be spending time with that book. Great—now you have another reason to focus. *GMAT Foundations of Verbal* covers all three Verbal problem types (Sentence Correction, Critical Reasoning, and Reading Comprehension), all of which come into play on the AWA essay. You need the parts of speech and other grammatical principles to strengthen the sentences you write. You need to spot missing assumptions and analyze other logical flaws to write an effective essay about a flawed argument. Finally, the better you *read* this kind of text (as in an RC passage), the better you can *write* this kind of text.

So focus on Verbal basics to build skill for the essay.

Step 2: Read and Write Summaries of High-Quality Articles in English

Find good source material. Use publications such as the *Economist*, the *Smithsonian*, the *Atlantic*, and the *New Yorker*. For daily newspapers, try the *New York Times*, the *Wall Street Journal*, the *Washington Post*, and the *Financial Times*. Go get *Scientific American*, the *Journal of American History*, the *Harvard Business Review*, or the *McKinsey Quarterly*. Pick up an alumni magazine from a top university. Visit MIT's Open-CourseWare site (ocw.mit.edu) to pick a course you find interesting and read materials from the syllabus.

Take note of sentences that strike you. Pick apart the core and examine how the author added modifiers or other bits of nuance and richness to the sentence. If you spot a particularly great sentence, you may even want to recopy it to solidify it in your brain.

If you get really ambitious, you can *rewrite* a piece, summarizing it or playing with language in some other way.

Step 3: Do a Few Sample Essays From the *Official Guide*

Pick a prompt at random. Give yourself 30 minutes and type an essay into a bare-bones word processor, as described earlier.

Now, without the pressure of time, analyze and rewrite each sentence in your essay. How could you have phrased your thoughts more precisely and more expressively? What words could you have chosen differently? How would you restructure the sentence?

At first, focus on polishing only the ideas that you were able to generate under time pressure. This way, the next time you have similar thoughts (as you will on other essays), the corresponding sentences will more easily and quickly coalesce.

Next, look for small gaps that you could close by adding material. Could you bulk up any existing sentences? What additional refinements could you add as modifiers? Could you provide better navigation and logical flow with signal words?

Finally, look for big gaps and other wholesale alterations. Did you miss any key flaws in the argument? If so, which kinds? Write and polish sentences corresponding to these flaws. Is there anything you'd cut or otherwise change drastically? If so, what?

Step 4: Learn to Type Faster

The faster and more easily you can type, the less brainpower you'll need for typing—and the more you can use on thinking and writing. If you type slowly, then your brain runs far ahead of your fingers and you lose your train of thought. In contrast, if you can get your thoughts down in near real time, you will simply write better.

Longer essays get higher scores, by and large. But that's far from the only reason to learn to type for real. If you spend more than 20 minutes a day at a computer keyboard, the time you invest in learning to type quickly by touch (without looking at the keys) will pay off more than any other investment you could possibly make.

Take a touch-typing course. There are many free resources on the web; google "learn to type" and see what you find.

Introduction to Integrated Reasoning

In This Chapter

- The Four Types of Prompts
- Table Analysis
- Graphics Interpretation
- Multi-Source Reasoning
- Two-Part Analysis
- IR Connections to Quant and Verbal
- How to Tackle IR: Understand–Plan–Solve

In this chapter, you will learn the basics about the four Integrated Reasoning (IR) problem types, as well as the ways in which the content in the IR section overlaps with the content in the Quant and Verbal sections of the GMAT and EA. You'll also learn Understand–Plan–Solve (UPS), a process you'll use to tackle every IR problem.

CHAPTER 3 Introduction to Integrated Reasoning

The Integrated Reasoning (IR) section is one of four sections on the GMAT and Executive Assessment (EA) exams. On the GMAT, it appears either second or third in the test order, depending on which order you choose at the beginning of the exam:

Option #1	Essay	IR	Quant	Verbal
Option #2	Quant	Verbal	IR	Essay
Option #3	Verbal	Quant	IR	Essay

On the EA, the IR section appears first, followed by the Verbal section and then the Quant section. (There is only one test order on the EA.)

As the name implies, Integrated Reasoning asks you to do both math and verbal analysis as you answer the 12 problems in the section. The good news: The quant and reasoning skills are the same ones that you're already studying for the Quant and Verbal sections of either exam. You do have some new skills to learn, though. Most IR problems have formats unique to this section of the test, including fill-in-the-blank statements, true/false statements, and other multipart formats.

Scoring on the GMAT

On the GMAT, the Integrated Reasoning section is scored separately from the rest of the test; your IR score does not affect your score on any other section. The IR score goes from 1 to 8 in integer increments; the lowest score is 1 and the highest score is 8.

As with the Quant and Verbal sections of the GMAT, you must answer IR problems in the order they appear; you must answer all parts of each problem, even if you have to guess, and you cannot go back to a problem you've already answered. However, unlike the Quant and Verbal sections of this test, the IR section is *not* adaptive, so your IR score is driven primarily by how many of the 12 problems you answer correctly, with slight adjustments for differences in problem difficulty.

Most schools weight the IR score more lightly than the Quant and Verbal scores in their admissions decisions. The mean score is between a 4 and a 5; for most schools, it's generally considered good enough to beat the mean. Aim for a score of 6 to give yourself a bit of leeway to fall short and still score a 5. (Of course, if IR is a strength for you, feel free to go for a higher score!)

Most of the major consulting and investment banking firms ask for GMAT scores when recruiting students from a master's program, and some do look at the IR score. If you hope to be hired by one of these firms, it's a good idea to aim for a score of 7 or 8 on the IR section.

Scoring on the EA

On the Executive Assessment, the Total score is equally weighted among your Integrated Reasoning, Verbal, and Quant subscores. For this test, you will want to focus your time and attention across all three sections relatively equally.

IR might even be a bit more important than the other two sections. On the EA, you will do the IR section first, and your performance on this section will determine your starting difficulty level for the subsequent Verbal and Quant sections of the test. (You'll learn more about this in Chapter 8.)

Overall, schools that take the EA aren't looking for the very high Total scores that people usually want on the GMAT. Since this test is relatively new, the standards are changing more quickly over time, but most programs find scores in the 150–160 range acceptable.

Whether you are taking the GMAT or the EA, do your research. First, check the school's website to see whether it publishes average scores for either exam. If it doesn't, ask the admissions department yourself.

Content

Most business schools use case studies to teach some or even most topics. Cases are true histories of difficult business situations; they include vast amounts of real information—both quantitative and verbal/logical—that you must sort through and analyze to glean insights and make decisions.

The IR section is designed to mirror two key aspects of case analysis that the Quant and Verbal sections of the GMAT and Executive Assessment don't address:

1. Math–verbal integration
2. The flood of real-world data

Problems on the Quant section of the test typically give you only what you need in order to solve and no more; the numbers often simplify cleanly, leaving you with an integer solution. In addition, the Quant section does not typically incorporate logical reasoning or other verbal skills, although it does require you to translate words into math. On the Verbal section, while Critical Reasoning (CR) and Reading Comprehension (RC) problems do include some extraneous information, they require only light mathematical understanding on occasion.

In contrast, IR may give you giant tables or graphics of ugly numbers or complex situations—but you'll never actually use most of the information (much like data in the real world). Further, you'll have to integrate the quant concepts with the kind of reasoning and analysis more typically found on the Verbal section of the exam.

In short, the IR section seeks to measure your ability to do case analysis in business school. Preparing for this section will be a challenge, but that work will actually help prepare you for grad school.

The Four Types of Prompts

Think of the layout of IR problems as similar to Reading Comprehension in the Verbal section: You're given a **Prompt** (or upfront information to process, similar to the RC passage), and you use that information to answer several questions.

Similarly, any IR problem will consist of two halves: a prompt and one or more questions associated with that prompt. The prompt is the collection of information you'll use to answer the question(s). On the IR section of both the GMAT and the Executive Assessment, you'll see 10 different prompts, accompanied by a total of 12 questions.

There are four types of IR prompts:

1. Table Analysis (aka Table)

2. Graphical Interpretation (aka Graph)

3. Multi-Source Reasoning (aka MSR)

4. Two-Part Analysis (aka Two-Part)

Table, Graph, and Two-Part prompts always have just one associated question. That is, for each Table prompt, you'll answer one question, and the same is true for each Graph prompt and each Two-Part prompt.

The MSR prompt, though, works like a full RC problem set: A single prompt typically comes with three associated questions. So that's how you will have only 10 prompts for 12 total questions.

The mix of questions on the IR section can vary. Here's one common mix of questions:

Prompt type	Total # of problems	Details
Table	2	2 prompts with 1 question each
Graph	3	3 prompts with 1 question each
MSR	3	1 prompt with 3 questions
Two-Part	4	4 prompts with 1 question each

Got all of that? Wait, there's one more thing to know. Most of those individual questions are multipart: You have to answer more than one thing for each question. The multipart questions all have either two or three parts that make up the full question.

Annoyed now? Yes, IR is complex. So is the real world! Once you gain some experience with IR, it will start to seem normal.

Table Analysis

The Table Analysis (Table) prompt is made up of two things: a sortable table and some additional text—also known as a **Blurb**—that gives you context about the information contained in the table. The blurb can be quite basic (e.g., a title); other times, the blurb may contain information necessary to answer the associated question.

The table will always appear on the left-hand side of the screen, and the question will always appear on the right-hand side. The blurb is sometimes above the table and sometimes above the question. In this example, the blurb is above the table:

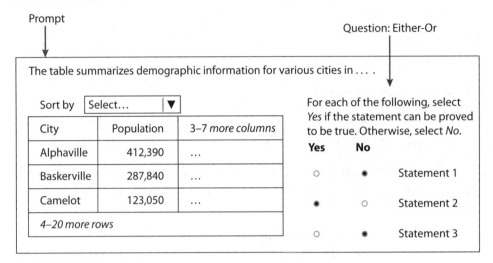

You will be able to sort the table by its columns; doing so will usually help you to save time and minimize careless mistakes. As you'll learn later in this guide, don't even think about trying to solve a Table problem without first considering the best sort to use.

Table prompts are always accompanied by one **Either-Or** question with three parts. The three parts will be in the form of three statements for which you will choose *either* the answer in the first column *or* the answer in the second column. In the example shown above, the choice is either Yes or No.

One more thing: There is no partial credit on the test. In order to get credit for the problem, you'll have to answer all three parts of the question correctly.

This has implications for test strategy. If you realize, for example, that you can answer one statement but you have no idea how to do the other two, then your best move might be to guess on all three and move on. Alternatively, if you feel confident that you can answer two parts in reasonable time but don't know how to do the third, you would likely still want to do that problem. A guess on the third part will still give you a 50/50 chance of answering the entire question correctly.

Essentially, the IR section is setting up the kinds of strategic decisions people have to make in the business world every day. How risky are the risks and how big are the rewards? You will often have to decide to let go of one business opportunity because you're betting that there will be some better opportunity down the line.

Graphics Interpretation

Graphics Interpretation (Graph) problems will present you with some kind of a graphic—anything from a classic pie chart or bar graph to some kind of unusual diagram created specifically for this test.

First, you'll see the graph or diagram and then you'll have a blurb describing the visual. As with tables, the blurb may just describe the visual or it may provide additional information that you'll need to use to answer the question. Here is an example:

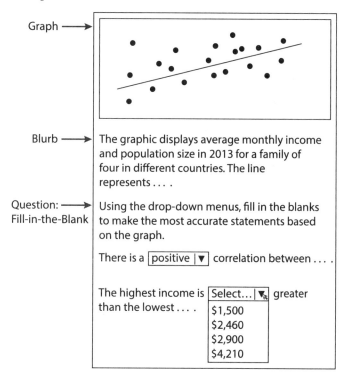

Graph problems are accompanied by a **Fill-in-the-Blank** question with two separate parts to complete. You'll be given one or two sentences with two drop-down menus placed somewhere in the text, offering you multiple-choice options to fill in the blanks. You may have anywhere from three to five answer choices for each blank, and you will need to answer both parts correctly in order to earn credit for the given problem.

As the image shows, the answers could be numerical or in word form. Because you cannot see the multiple-choice answer options automatically, it's important to train yourself to click the drop-down arrows and view the answers very early in your process—before you even begin to try to understand the graph or process the statements. Knowing the form of the answers will help you to decide what approach to use when solving the problem.

Multi-Source Reasoning

Like Reading Comprehension prompts, Multi-Source Reasoning prompts will present you with a bunch of text along with a set of questions based on that text. Unlike RC passages, however, the information in MSR can include tables, charts, graphs, or other diagrams along with the text, and all of the information provided is spread across two or three tabs that can only be viewed one at a time. In order to answer the accompanying questions, you must integrate information from different tabs—many people dislike MSR for this reason.

MSR will feel like an RC passage: The prompt will stay on the left-hand side of the screen the whole time, but you will have a series of different questions appear on the right-hand side of the screen. Most of the time, you'll have a total of three separate accompanying questions. Here is an example:

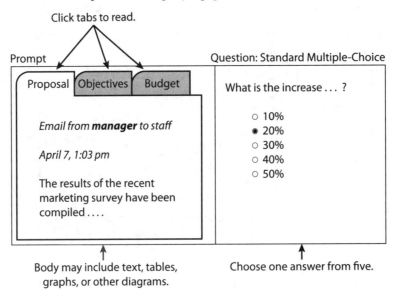

The image above is an example of one type of question for an MSR prompt. Here's an example of the other type of question, shown with the same prompt:

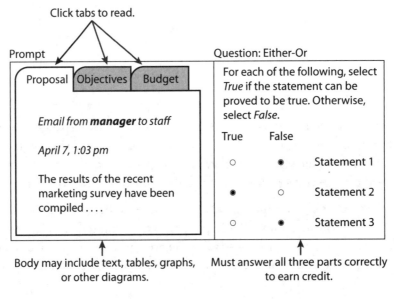

MSR questions always come in one of these two forms: standard multiple-choice or the same either-or form that you already saw with Table problems.

Each separate screen is its own question. Anything that appears on the same screen is a single (possibly multipart) question. The second example shows one either-or question with three parts (three statements); all three parts must be answered correctly in order to earn the point for that question.

Since there are three separate questions for an MSR prompt, you have the chance to earn three separate points, one for each question.

Most often, just one of the questions will be in typical multiple-choice format with five answer choices, among which you select one. This is the only type of IR question that is not multipart.

The other two MSR questions are usually either-or questions (each with three parts). These will work the same way either-or questions do for Tables, and you can use the same approaches to answer them.

Two-Part Analysis

Superficially, Two-Part Analysis (Two-Part) problems look very similar to multiple-choice problems from the Quant and Verbal sections of the test—until you get to the answers.

The example below fairly closely resembles a standard Quant problem, though as the name implies, you'll have to answer two questions (one in each column). The prompt appears first, typically in paragraph form, and the question is always below that:

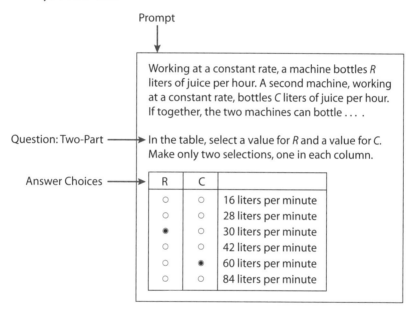

Finally, you'll see a little table that contains your available answer choices in the right-hand column, along with two labeled columns on the left side. Those first two columns will be the two parts of the question you need to answer. Notice that the answer choices are the same for both parts; this will always be the case. As with all multipart questions, you'll need to answer all parts correctly in order to earn credit on Two-Part problems.

Two-Parts can also closely resemble classic Critical Reasoning problems—perhaps they'll ask you to both strengthen and weaken an argument. You may even see a logic-based problem, in which you're given a series of constraints and asked a scenario-based question. For example, you may be given various criteria for setting a time for a meeting (times that certain people are or are not available, people who must attend versus those whose attendance is optional, and so on), and then be asked to select the time that permits the maximum number of attendees—without leaving out anyone whose attendance is mandatory.

Two-Part prompts will often feel the least real-world and the most standardized-test-like of the IR question types. Two-Parts tend to be primarily quant-based, verbal-based, or logic-based; they don't often mix the three topic areas.

IR Connections to Quant and Verbal

The Integrated Reasoning section tests many of the same facts and skills tested on other sections of the GMAT and Executive Assessment.

Quant

For both Quant and IR, you'll need to know the same formulas, facts, and rules. The general problem-solving techniques you learn for the Quant section will also work on the IR section, but there is one key difference: The IR section includes lots of extra information, so you'll need to decide what to pay attention to and what to ignore. By contrast, problems in the Quant section rarely give information that you don't use.

Though any part of Quant is fair game on the IR section of the test, IR does emphasize two main content areas:

1. Fractions, Decimals, Percents, and Ratios

2. Statistics

You can find an overview of the two main Quant content areas in Appendix B of this guide. For more in-depth study of these and other topics, see the *GMAT All the Quant* guide.

A basic on-screen calculator is available during the IR section (but *not* during the Quant section). The calculator can be a blessing and a curse; it's important to learn when and how to use this tool (and when not to use it).

In the test screen window, click the link in the upper left corner to pull up the calculator. Note that the calculator will float above the problem on the screen; you can move it around, but you cannot click on the problem to answer the question while the calculator is still open.

The calculator includes the following limited functions:

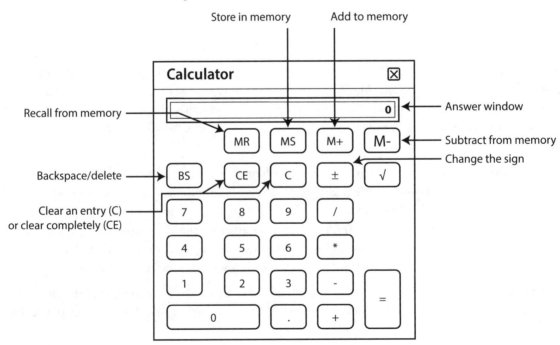

Have you ever panicked on a math problem during a test, picked up a calculator, and punched in some numbers, hoping inspiration would strike? If you ever find yourself doing this during the IR section, stop immediately, pick any random answer, and move on. The calculator is not a substitute for the actual solution process.

That said, don't hesitate to pull up the calculator when you do need it. The Quant section of the test often provides numbers that work pretty cleanly in calculations; the IR section, by contrast, won't hesitate to give you messy numbers. As long as you know what steps you want to take, the calculator can be a very helpful tool.

Verbal

The IR and Verbal sections overlap on reasoning and comprehension skills; the IR section does not include any grammar.

Some IR problems look very similar to Critical Reasoning problems. For instance, a Two-Part problem may ask you to find an assumption made by the argument and a flaw in the argument's reasoning.

CR, RC, and IR all have Inference problems, and you can use the same general approach for all three types.

The Executive Mindset

In order to do well on any test, you need to know how that test works. The Executive Mindset section at the beginning of this guide introduced you to the type of mindset that you want to take into both your studies and the exam itself.

Most people cannot answer all 12 problems in the 30 minutes given for the section; there is simply too much information thrown at you to answer each problem in an average of just 2.5 minutes. The vast majority of test-takers, then, will need to guess on at least one IR problem—and probably closer to two to four.

You'll learn more later in this guide about how to know when to bail (guess immediately and move on); just know for now that you will need to do this, whether you are taking the GMAT or the Executive Assessment.

GMAT Scoring

As you work through the section, you will earn points based upon the number of full problems you answer correctly. A full problem is one that appears on its own separate screen; it will have one, two, or three parts to answer. If there are multiple parts, you must answer all parts correctly in order to earn any credit for that problem.

While the exact scoring scale has never been published, research has uncovered the fact that you can miss a number of problems and still earn a good score on the test.

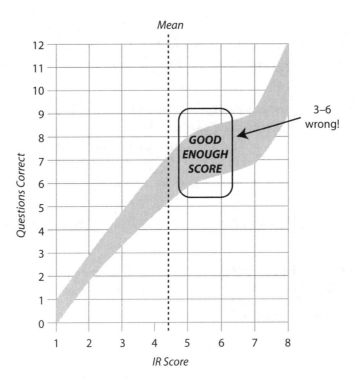

As shown in the graph above, the mean score is between a 4 and a 5, so it's recommended to aim for a score of 5 or higher. If you are applying to an especially competitive school, aim for a 6 or higher. (And if you would like to apply for internships or jobs with the top management consulting or investment banking firms, aim for a 7 or 8 on IR.)

If you're aiming for a score of 6 or higher, plan to bail (guess very quickly) on 2 problems in the section. You'll be able to spend an average of 3 minutes on the remaining 10 problems—and you'll be able to answer some of these incorrectly and still hit your target score.

If you're going for a score of 5, plan to bail on three problems in the section. You'll have nearly 3.5 minutes to spend on the remaining nine problems. Likewise, you'll be able to answer some incorrectly and still hit the target.

EA Scoring

Because the Executive Assessment is a relatively new exam, not as much is known about the scoring. The scoring range for the IR section is 0–20 points, but on the official practice test, someone who answers every single question correctly earns only 18 points, so that appears to be the practical upper limit. (The same is true for the Quant and Verbal sections of the EA.)

If you can hit a score of 10 on each of the three sections, your Total score will be 150, which is the minimum score many schools say they want to see. If you plan to bail on two or three problems, as recommended, you can still miss two to three additional problems and score at or close to a 10.

In Sum

By the time you're done studying for Integrated Reasoning, you should know two things:

1. Your weakest problem types and content areas

2. Your target score

You'll bail quickly on two or three harder problems in your weaker areas and allocate that saved time to other problems in the section.

As you work through the rest of this guide, you'll learn more about how and when to bail. While you study, keep in mind that you need to have a good handle on your own strengths and weaknesses in order to make good decisions about when to move on. (This is true for the whole test, not just IR!)

How to Tackle IR: Understand–Plan–Solve

Here is a universal 3-step process for Integrated Reasoning:

Step 1: Understand the prompt and question

Step 2: Plan your approach

Step 3: Solve the problem

At first glance, the process might seem pretty simple. Most test-takers, though, jump straight to solving and pay minimal attention to the earlier steps. If you want to get through IR with a minimum of stress and a good score, follow the process!

Step 1: Understand the Prompt and Question

Your first goal is just to comprehend the given information.

First, glance at the entire problem. What type is it? Do any clues jump out at you that tell you what this is testing overall? For example, if you see a pie chart, then you know you've got a Graph problem and there's a good chance you'll need to do some work with percentages. If you see any type of problem with answer choices in sentence form, then you know you've got a more verbal-focused problem.

Next, as you scan the given data, ask yourself *what* and *so what* questions:

What **is this?**

- What is the title or accompanying text indicating?
- What is in this tab, this row, or this column?
- What kind of graph is this and what do these points on the graph represent?
- What kinds of numbers are these—percents or other relative values? Or absolute quantities, such as dollars or barrels?

So what **about this?**

- How is this information organized?
- Why is this part here? What purpose does it serve, relative to everything else?
- How does it all fit together? What connections can you draw?

Finally, articulate the question to yourself in your own words. The wording is sometimes meant to trick you. For instance, the question might imply that you must use an advanced, time-consuming solution process when a much faster shortcut exists. You do have access to an on-screen calculator, but sometimes you can estimate aggressively and don't need to pull up the calculator at all.

Some people like to read the question first, before reading the prompt. If you like to do this, that's fine—just don't skip either step!

Step 2: Plan Your Approach

Next, you'll need to figure out what to *do* with the given information in order to solve the problem:

- What do you have to look up? Which portions should you reread?
- What pieces of information do you have to combine?
- What formulas will you need to use?
- What shortcuts can you use? Can you eyeball a figure or a list of numbers? Can you estimate?
- How should you organize your work?

You won't be able to determine every last step of your plan before you start to solve, but do think about the kind of information you need and how to organize it. Also think about the types of calculations you will need to do or steps you will need to take.

Step 3: Solve the Problem

Now, execute your plan of attack. If you've done the first two steps well, you'll make this step easier for yourself. And if you realize that you don't really understand some aspect of the prompt or question, or you can't devise a decent plan of attack, then you know that you should guess and move on. Save that time and mental energy for some other problem in this section!

When you do decide to move to the final step and solve, think about how to organize your work before you dive in. Be methodical; write notes and calculations clearly to minimize the chance of careless mistakes. Finally, if you get stuck at any step along the way, don't dwell. Go back and try to unstick yourself once. If you're still stuck, guess and move on to the next question. Remember: You can get a lot wrong and still get a good score!

As you work your way through the rest of this guide, you'll learn how to apply the Understand–Plan–Solve process to each of the four IR problem types.

Table Analysis

In This Chapter

- UPS for Tables

- Sort, Eyeball, and Estimate

- Review and Improve on Tables

In this chapter, you will learn how to apply the Understand–Plan–Solve (UPS) process to Table problems. You'll also learn how to apply the SEE (sort, eyeball, estimate) approach to Tables.

CHAPTER 4 Table Analysis

Table Analysis (Table) problems, unsurprisingly, require you to analyze tables of information.

The table appears on the left side of the screen; the question appears on the right side of the screen. Table prompts are always accompanied by one three-part **Either-Or** question (e.g., true/false, yes/no).

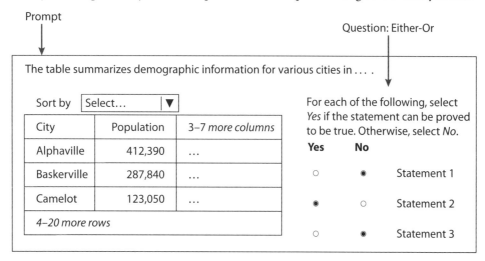

The table can be presented alone or with an associated blurb, which can range from a simple title to a full paragraph of information that you must understand in order to fully process the data in the table. The blurb is sometimes placed on the left side, above the table, and sometimes on the right side, above the question.

You'll be able to sort the data by column, but if you're an experienced Excel user, you'll find the sorting very limited. The sorts will always be ascending, and you can perform only one sort at a time (no secondary sorts).

UPS for Tables

As discussed in the Introduction to Integrated Reasoning chapter earlier in this guide, you'll use the UPS process to solve all IR problems, including Tables. UPS stands for Understand the prompt and question, Plan, and Solve. (If you skipped that section of Chapter 3, you may want to go back and read it now.)

Table problems usually have a quantitative focus, often testing general Statistics (mean, median, standard deviation, range, correlation, and so on) and Fractions, Decimals, Percents, and Ratios.

Take a look at the following Table problem:

> The table displays data from the different divisions of Company X in 2011. Market shares are computed by dividing Company X's total sales (in dollars) for that division by the total sales (in dollars) made by all companies selling products in that category. Market shares are separately calculated for the world (global market share) and for the United States (U.S. market share). Ranks are based on Company X's position relative to other companies competing in the same market.

Division	Global market share	Global market rank	U.S. market share	U.S. market rank
Agriculture & Food	8%	6	12%	4
Health Care & Medical	12%	4	18%	2
Household Goods & Personal Care	5%	5	10%	4
Performance Plastics	30%	1	26%	1
Water & Process Solutions	19%	1	26%	1

Select *Yes* if the statement can be proved true for Company X in 2011 based on the information provided in the table. Otherwise, select *No*.

Yes	No	
O	O	There is a positive correlation between global market share and U.S. market share.
O	O	The same division of Company X is the median of Company X's five divisions by both U.S. market rank and global market rank.
O	O	The Performance Plastics division had greater market share in at least one other country than it had in the United States.

Step 1: Understand the Prompt and Question

The table and the blurb accompanying it are the prompt; focus on that first.

To understand the prompt, you're going to do three things: glance, read, and jot.

First, **Glance** at the table title (if applicable) and at the column and row headers. In this case, there is no title. The first column shows *divisions* that appear to be categories for different types of products. The next two columns provide global market data, and the final two provide U.S. market data. That data has to do with market share (in percent form) and market rank.

Next, **Read** the blurb (if any) given with the table. If the blurb explains specific parts of the table, examine the relevant parts as you read:

- In this case, the blurb indicates that the table contains data about the divisions of one specific company. Now you have the full context for the first column of the table.

- Next, the blurb explains how market share is calculated. Glance again to reinforce the message: The *Global market share* column shows market share for the entire global market and the *U.S. market share* column shows market share for just the U.S. They are both in percentage form. (Note: The U.S. market is a subset of the global market, since the global market is comprised of the markets of all countries.)

- Finally, the blurb indicates that the table shows how each division ranks against all other companies in that geographic region; again, glance at the table to reinforce the message.

Time to **Jot**. Take another glance over the full table to make sure you know the kind of data you have and how it is presented, then consider what you want to jot down. Your goal is not to make an inventory of everything you read. Rather, jotting at this stage can help to reinforce the major messages and keep you oriented properly as you try to solve the problem.

In this case, you might jot down something like this:

> Global vs. U.S.
> Share % + Rank for each

If you are not completely sure that you fully understand what you just reviewed, pick a cell or group of cells in the table and then articulate to yourself what the value or values represent. For example, the Household Goods & Personal Care division has a global market share of 5% and is ranked fifth in the global market in that category. There are four other companies that outrank this division of Company X in the global market (i.e., four other companies each make at least 5% of the global sales in that category).

If you can do this, great! Move on to the question. If you can't, consider whether you want to do this problem at all. If not, guess randomly—and immediately—and move on.

It is possible that a table blurb will contain complex additional information—that is, information about something other than the specific data in the table. For instance, in this example, the blurb provides some extra detail regarding how those numbers are calculated.

When this happens, you may not be able to fully understand or process this information until later. That's okay. You don't have to bail now if you don't understand that type of information. As long as you understand the basic information contained in the table, keep going.

Let's move to the question. It will first provide directions and then give you a box with three statements. Here is the question text for this problem again:

> Select *Yes* if the statement can be proved true for Company X in 2011 based on the information provided in the table. Otherwise, select *No*.

Yes	No	
○	○	There is a positive correlation between global market share and U.S. market share.
○	○	The same division of Company X is the median of Company X's five divisions by both U.S. market rank and global market rank.
○	○	The Performance Plastics division had greater market share in at least one other country than it had in the United States.

This is an either-or problem; Table prompts always use this problem type. You will be asked to select one of two answers in either X or Y form: in this case, either *Yes* or *No*.

Three statements accompany the question; your task is to choose a single option for each statement. In order to earn credit for this problem, you have to answer all three statements correctly.

As with the prompt, your first goal is to understand the question asked. In this case, the question is whether you can *prove* each statement *true* based on the information provided. The *for Company X in 2011* language is given in order to avoid having to specify those details in each statement; they aren't going to try to trick you by asking a question about a random Company Y or a different year, for which no data is given, just to see whether you're paying attention.

Next, glance through the three statements.

First, are they more quant-based (you're asked about some actual math concept) or verbal/analytic-based (you're asked to infer or otherwise analyze in a way that doesn't involve computation)?

The first statement mentions correlation, a quant topic, but the other two are focused on your ability to read the table properly, so they are more verbal or analytical in nature.

Also note that the three statements look fairly different, so you will probably need to solve each one separately. This is the case most of the time on Table problems, but occasionally the statements are very similar and can be solved using the same process—sometimes even simultaneously.

Next, read the first statement. If it seems straightforward, go ahead to the next step in the process. If not, skip that statement for now and read the second one. You never need to solve the statements in order; you can start with whichever one seems easiest to you. (If you read all three statements and realize you don't want to start with any of them, guess immediately and move on.)

Step 2: Plan Your Approach

Assume that you decide to start with the first statement:

Yes	No	
O	O	There is a positive correlation between global market share and U.S. market share.

First, remind yourself of any math concepts, formulas, or rules you might need. In this case, what does *positive correlation* mean?

Two sets of data have a positive correlation when the two sets of numbers increase together or decrease together. For example, the age of a tree and the circumference of its trunk have a positive correlation: As age increases, so does the circumference of the trunk.

Next, on a Table problem, it is usually the case that sorting the table in some way will make it easier for you to find the answer. What kind of sort would be useful in this case?

The two relevant columns are *Global market share* and *U.S. market share*. Should you sort by the former or the latter? Sometimes, this will be obvious. Other times, you may have to think about this a bit or even try a couple of different sorts.

In this case, you can sort by either column. You'll be looking to see whether they "go in the same direction"—that is, they both generally increase or they both generally decrease.

Step 3: Solve the Problem

Here's the table sorted by *Global market share*:

Division	Global market share	Global market rank	U.S. market share	U.S. market rank
Household Goods & Personal Care	5%	5	10%	4
Agriculture & Food	8%	6	12%	4
Health Care & Medical	12%	4	18%	2
Water & Process Solutions	19%	1	26%	1
Performance Plastics	30%	1	26%	1

As global market share increases, U.S. market share does increase, indicating a positive correlation.

The answer to the first statement is *Yes*.

Evaluate the second and third statements in the same manner, repeating the Plan and Solve steps. Here's the second statement:

Yes	No	
○	○	The same division of Company X is the median of Company X's five divisions by both U.S. market rank and global market rank.

The median for five divisions would be the division in the third position when the numbers are placed in increasing order. You can sort either by global rank or by U.S. rank, your choice. Here is the sort by *U.S. market rank*:

Division	Global market share	Global market rank	U.S. market share	U.S. market rank
Performance Plastics	30%	1	26%	1
Water & Process Solutions	19%	1	26%	1
Health Care & Medical	12%	4	18%	2
Agriculture & Food	8%	6	12%	4
Household Goods & Personal Care	5%	5	10%	4

The Health Care & Medical division falls into the third-highest position for the U.S. rankings. Now, take a look at the *Global market rank* column. In a longer or more jumbled list, you might have to sort a second time by this column. In this case, though, the numbers are almost in order already; only the 5 and the 6 would need to be swapped. The Health Care & Medical division is again in the third position of the five divisions within Company X.

The answer to the second statement is *Yes*.

Here is the third statement:

Yes	No	
○	○	The Performance Plastics division had greater market share in at least one other country than it had in the United States.

In this case, you don't need to sort any columns; you can answer using just the Performance Plastics row:

Division	Global market share	Global market rank	U.S. market share	U.S. market rank
Performance Plastics	30%	1	26%	1

U.S. market share is 26% and global market share is 30%. In other words, this division had a higher market share globally than in the United States.

The U.S. market is a subset of the global market, so U.S. sales contribute to the company's global sales. What is the relationship between global market share and market share in just one country?

If the U.S. market were the global market—that is, these products were sold nowhere else in the world—the division's U.S. market share and global market share would be identical. The U.S. and global market shares are not the same, though, so there must be at least one other country in which the Performance Plastics division has sales.

Next, imagine that the division has 26% market share in every country where these products are sold. If that were the case, the company would have exactly 26% of the global market share as well. Its global share is greater, though—it has 30% of the market share globally. So it must have a greater share of the market somewhere other than the United States.

That scenario is what the third statement says: Company X's global market share, at 30%, is larger than its U.S. market share, so it must have a greater market share in at least one other country than it does in the United States.

The answer to the third statement is *Yes*.

The answers are as follows:

Yes	No	
◉	○	There is a positive correlation between global market share and U.S. market share.
◉	○	The same division of Company X is the median of Company X's five divisions by both U.S. market rank and global market rank.
◉	○	The Performance Plastics division had greater market share in at least one other country than it had in the United States.

Sort, Eyeball, and Estimate

On any Table problem, don't do any work at all until you've considered how to **SEE: Sort, Eyeball**, and **Estimate**. These steps will save you a lot of time and mental effort on the exam.

Try this problem:

> The table presents the Q1 medical equipment sales figures for 9 regional sales teams and the forecasted changes in sales for each quarter (relative to the prior quarter). Q1 figures are in thousands of dollars.

Sales team	Q1 sales (in thousands)	Forecast		
		Q2 (change from Q1)	Q3 (change from Q2)	Q4 (change from Q3)
A	$ 902	−13.2%	8.6%	−8.3%
B	$1,301	−10.4%	−11.6%	−6.0%
C	$1,793	17.0%	−7.4%	13.2%
D	$ 877	−6.8%	−5.1%	−4.6%
E	$3,866	1.2%	3.5%	3.7%
F	$2,576	4.9%	4.2%	1.4%
G	$2,140	−5.4%	3.3%	2.2%
H	$3,214	15.6%	8.5%	−7.6%
I	$4,325	12.4%	−12.4%	16.8%

> For each of the following statements, select *True* if the statement can be shown to be true using the information provided. Otherwise, select *False*.

True	False	
○	○	According to the forecasts, the team with the median sales in Q1 will also have the median sales in Q2.
○	○	Of the teams that are projected to see a quarterly increase in Q3, more than half are expected to see an additional quarterly increase in Q4.
○	○	The number of teams projected to see a quarterly decrease in both Q2 and Q3 is greater than the number of teams projected to see a quarterly decrease in both Q3 and Q4.

How did it go? Before continuing to read here, go back over your work to look for opportunities to answer any of the statements more efficiently. Pay close attention to any steps that seemed cumbersome; can you brainstorm any ideas to streamline or entirely avoid that part?

Step 1: Understand the Prompt and Question

The blurb is pretty basic; it just explains what's in the table.

Interestingly, actual quantities are given only in the Q1 column. The other three are all percentage increases or decreases from the immediately preceding quarter (the column to the left). Pick a row and follow the numbers to the right to see how they work.

How about row G? This team had Q1 sales of $2,140,000. Since all given numbers are in thousands, you can ignore the final three zeros and just call it $2,140. In Q2, sales are projected to decline: The forecast for Team G is a negative percent change. If you wanted to find the forecasted sales figure for Q2, you would either take 5.4% of the Q1 figure and subtract or you would multiply the Q1 figure by $(100 - 5.4)\% = 94.6\%$. Sales are projected to increase in Q3 and Q4, though: The forecast for Team G is a positive percent change in both quarters.

So you can see at a glance whether the team is predicted to do better or worse than the immediately previous quarter, based on whether the percentage change is positive or negative—but you would have to crunch the numbers to know the actual sales figures for Q2, Q3, and Q4.

4

Mini Math Lesson

Percentages do funny things. For example, in the final row, Sales Team I is forecast to have a 12.4% increase in Q2 and a 12.4% decrease in Q3. Does that mean that their sales figure in Q3 ends up back where it was in Q1, at $4,325K?

Think about that. If you're not sure, go ahead and calculate the steps to see what happens.

First, if you take any number and increase it by a certain percentage, then decrease the resulting number by the same percentage, you will never end up back at the same starting point (unless your starting point was 0 or your percentage was 0%). Why?

Try some real numbers to see. If you have $100 and increase by $20, you'll have $120. Now, take that new figure and decrease by 20%: $120 − $24 = $96.

It will always be the case that 20% of a smaller number is less than 20% of a greater number, so when you increase by a certain percentage and then decrease by that same percentage, you'll always end up lower than where you started. The same is true for Sales Team I: For Q3, they are forecast to have sales below their starting point of $4,325K.

By the way, do you think Team G did better or worse in Q4 than in Q1? Make your best guess, then do the math to check. The answer is at the end of this section.

Back to the problem. Here's the question stem again:

> For each of the following statements, select True if the statement can be shown to be true using the information provided. Otherwise, select False.

Essentially, can the statement be proven true using the data in the table? If so, call that one true. If you can't prove it true *using the given data*, call it false.

Here's the first statement:

True	False	
◯	◯	According to the forecasts, the team with the median sales in Q1 will also have the median sales in Q2.

The statement says that the same team has the median sales in both Q1 and Q2.

Glance back up at the blurb; how many sales teams are there? Nine. (You don't have to count—the blurb says that there are nine teams. Always check the blurb first before you try to count the total number of rows; if it's a longer table, chances are the blurb will tell you.)

Step 2: Plan Your Approach

To find the median, the numbers have to be listed in order, so you're definitely going to sort this thing. Finding the median for Q1 will be easy, since the Q1 column shows the actual sales figures.

Q2, though, is trickier, as it shows only the percentage increase or decrease from Q1. You do have a calculator, so maybe you just have to calculate the forecasted sales for each sales team in Q2?

There are nine rows. That's a lot of work.

So stop! Don't do annoying math. This is why you Plan before you Solve. First, sort by Q1 sales to find that median, then examine the data to think about the best approach for the Q2 data.

Step 3: (Start to) Solve the Problem

Here's the table sorted by Q1 (and without Q3 or Q4, since they don't matter for this statement):

Sales team	Q1 sales (in thousands)	Q2 (change from Q1)
D	$ 877	−6.8%
A	$ 902	−13.2%
B	$1,301	−10.4%
C	$1,793	17.0%
G	$2,140	−5.4%
F	$2,576	4.9%
H	$3,214	15.6%
E	$3,866	1.2%
I	$4,325	12.4%

The median for Q1 is the fifth one from the top or the bottom: Team G.

Go back to your Plan stage for a minute and remind yourself of the question: Does Team G have the median for *both* Q1 and Q2? In other words, does Team G stay in the fifth position or does its position change?

Team G's sales will decrease a little bit, but not that much—a little over 5%. The numbers for each team are far enough apart that you can use benchmarks to estimate the change:

10% of $2,140 = $214
Half of that = 5% = $107
$2,140 − $107 ≈ $2,000

Next, eyeball the data to see which other teams *might* change positions relative to Team G. (To *eyeball* is to look and think logically about the data; you won't be doing any actual calculations, even at an estimation level.)

Teams D, A, and B are already below $2,000 in Q1 and they all decrease further, so they will still stay below Team G in the Q2 list. No need to calculate anything for them.

Team C, by contrast, increases, so it could jump past Team G. You might have to do some calculations, so jot down Team C on your scratch paper as a reminder.

Next, take a look at the teams that have Q1 sales greater than those of Team G. They are already higher than $2,000 and all four increase in Q2, so they will stay above Team G in that quarter.

The only possibility is that Team C will swap places with Team G. Eyeballing the data saves a lot of time that would have been wasted with unnecessary calculations!

Jot down the numbers you need, then figure out how to do the calculations. Finally, plug the calculations into your calculator to solve:

	Q1 value	Q2 % change	Q2 value (rounded)
Team C	1,793	+17.0%	$(1,793)(1 + 0.17) = \$2,098$
Team G	2,140	−5.4%	$(2,140)(1 − 0.054) = \$2,024$

Team C does indeed pass Team G in Q2, so Team C is now the team with the median sales volume. Is it *not* true that the same team is in the median position for both quarters.

The correct answer for statement 1 is *False*.

Here is statement 2:

True	False	
○	○	Of the teams that are projected to see a quarterly increase in Q3, more than half are expected to see an additional quarterly increase in Q4.

This time, the statement focuses on Q3 and Q4. When you see something like *of the teams that* (fall into a certain category), the statement is giving you a qualifier: It wants you to consider only a subset of the categories given in the table.

In this case, the desired subset is those teams that will have a Q3 increase. You don't technically have to sort in order to see which teams have positive percentages in Q3, but do so anyway. Sorting by Q3 will group those teams together so that you don't inadvertently include teams that you don't want.

Before you do that, though, jot down what the statement wants you to find. Here's one way to do that:

$$\text{Is } \frac{(\text{Q3 AND Q4}) + \%}{\text{Q3} + \% \text{ only}} > \frac{1}{2}?$$

Here's another:

Do >50% of teams that ↑ in Q3 *also* ↑ in Q4?

Note it in any way that makes sense to you. Here's the data sorted by the Q3 column:

Sales team	Q3 (change from Q2)	Q4 (change from Q3)
I	−12.4%	16.8%
B	−11.6%	−6.0%
C	−7.4%	13.2%
D	−5.1%	−4.6%
G	3.3%	2.2%
E	3.5%	3.7%
F	4.2%	1.4%
H	8.5%	−7.6%
A	8.6%	−8.3%

Only five of the teams will have a quarterly increase in Q3: Teams G, E, F, H, and A. Of just those teams, three also have an increase in Q4: Teams G, E, and F.

Therefore, three out of five of the teams increase in both quarters. This is greater than 50%, so this statement is true.

The correct answer for statement 2 is *True*.

Here is the third statement:

True	False	
○	○	The number of teams projected to see a quarterly decrease in both Q2 and Q3 is greater than the number of teams projected to see a quarterly decrease in both Q3 and Q4.

This is very similar to statement 2: You're looking for two adjacent quarters with the same trend. You have to do it for two groupings this time, not just one. Jot this down in a form that makes sense for you; here's one way to do that:

Is # (Q2 and Q3) ↓ more than # (Q3 and Q4) ↓ ?

Make sure to evaluate each part separately so that you don't, for example, mistakenly carry over Q2 data into the examination of Q3 and Q4. And you'll again minimize your chances of a careless error if you sort as you go. First, sort by Q2:

Sales team	Q2 (change from Q1)	Q3 (change from Q2)
A	−13.2%	8.6%
B	−10.4%	−11.6%
D	−6.8%	−5.1%
G	−5.4%	3.3%
E	1.2%	3.5%
F	4.9%	4.2%
I	12.4%	−12.4%
H	15.6%	8.5%
C	17.0%	−7.4%

Two teams are projected to have a decrease in both Q2 and Q3: Teams B and D.

Next, sort by Q3:

Sales team	Q3 (change from Q2)	Q4 (change from Q3)
I	−12.4%	16.8%
B	−11.6%	−6.0%
C	−7.4%	13.2%
D	−5.1%	−4.6%
G	3.3%	2.2%
E	3.5%	3.7%
F	4.2%	1.4%
H	8.5%	−7.6%
A	8.6%	−8.3%

Again, two teams are projected to have a decrease in both Q3 and Q4; Teams B and D again.

It is *not* the case that the number of teams with decreased sales in both Q2 and Q3 is greater than that in both Q3 and Q4.

The correct answer for statement 3 is *False*.

The answers are:

True	False	
○	◉	According to the forecasts, the team with the median sales in Q1 will also have the median sales in Q2.
◉	○	Of the teams that are projected to see a quarterly increase in Q3, more than half are expected to see an additional quarterly increase in Q4.
○	◉	The number of teams projected to see a quarterly decrease in both Q2 and Q3 is greater than the number of teams projected to see a quarterly decrease in both Q3 and Q4.

Whenever you have to solve a Table problem, don't do any real work until you consider how you can SEE (sort, eyeball, estimate) to save yourself time and effort. On this problem, all three of these strategies made a big difference for the first statement. For the other two statements, sorting saved a small amount of time and—perhaps more important—helped to minimize the chances of a careless error.

Don't hesitate to pop up the on-screen calculator when you need it; just make sure that you know what you need to calculate before you start punching in numbers. It's a good idea to write out the calculations you want to do before you start using the calculator.

4

Mini Math Lesson Redux

So, what happened with Team G?

Most people will guess that Team G ends up with greater sales in Q4 than in Q1...but it doesn't! Why do people think this and why are they wrong?

Nobody wants to do tedious calculations, so most people will just compare the percentages. Sales are forecast to decrease by 5.4% in Q2, but then increase by 3.3% and 2.2% in Q3 and Q4, respectively. That seems like a 5.5% increase, since 3.3% + 2.2% = 5.5%, and 5.5% is greater than 5.4%, right?

Maybe. Would you rather have 5.5% of $10 or 5.4% of $1,000,000?

Why?

Here's how the calculations play out:

$$Q1: \qquad\qquad\qquad 2{,}140$$
$$Q2: -5.4\% = (2{,}140)(1 - 0.054) = 2{,}024$$
$$Q3: +3.3\% = (2{,}024)(1 + 0.033) = 2{,}091$$
$$Q4: +2.2\% = (2{,}091)(1 + 0.022) = 2{,}137$$

Since the first step is a decrease, that lowers the base figure that Team G is working from. The forecast is for an increase of 3.3% in Q3, but the increase is calculated from a lower base (2,024) than the initial 5.6% was taken away from. The same is true for the 2.2% increase.

So, for the same reason that you would much rather have 5.4% of a greater number than 5.5% of a smaller one, Team G finished the year a bit lower than it started.

Alternatively, you could use the calculator to find the cumulative change for Q4 in one combined step: cumulative change from Q1 to Q4 = (0.946)(1.033)(1.022) = 0.9987 = 99.87%.

In other words, the Q4 sales forecast is 99.87% of the Q1 sales figure. This is less than 100%, so Q4 sales will be less than Q1 sales.

Review and Improve on Tables

The Understand–Plan–Solve process will help you both solve the problem and review your work afterwards. Do review the problem regardless of whether you got it right or wrong.

If you answer a question incorrectly—or aren't fully confident about something you answered correctly—review each step of the process. Did you overlook, misunderstand, or fail to comprehend any information in the prompt? Did you inadvertently answer a different question than the one that was asked? Was there a better way to approach the problem? Did you make any mistakes at the solution stage?

If you answer it correctly, ask yourself whether there are any opportunities to do it better next time. Where could you streamline any steps of the process? (Consider both time and mental energy.) What if it took a long time to solve and you don't see a way to make it faster—do you really want to do this on the real test? It might be better to guess quickly and spend your time elsewhere.

Grab a timer and give yourself approximately 3 minutes to try this problem:

> The table summarizes total sales information for a large production company for the first six months of 2014. The table also provides percent of total sales from the company's only three divisions (Electronics, Housewares, and Automotive). The company acquired the automotive division in March of that year.

2014 Monthly Sales by Product Line

Month	Total ($, thousands)	% Electronics	% Housewares	% Automotive
January	3,890	47.09	52.91	0.00
February	4,204	49.75	50.25	0.00
March	6,561	34.19	33.00	32.81
April	6,982	36.44	34.03	29.53
May	6,613	37.97	33.34	28.69
June	7,028	34.58	34.00	31.42

> For each of the following statements, select *Would help explain* if the statement would, if true, help explain some of the information in the table. Otherwise, select *Would not help explain*.

Would help explain	Would not help explain	
O	O	Consumer purchases of electronics typically drop just after the month of December, but they revive within two to three months.
O	O	Companies that have electronics, housewares, and automotive product lines tend to have higher total sales in housewares than do companies that sell only one or two of these product lines.
O	O	The housewares division took a $1.1 million loss in March due to an accounting change.

How did it go? Before reading the explanations below (or even checking whether you got it right), ask yourself whether you're generally happy with how things went. If you want to try any part of the problem again, go ahead; you don't need to time yourself, and you can look up anything you want elsewhere in this guide.

Then, take a look at the correct answers (scroll to the end of this section—the answers are not immediately below so that the question isn't "spoiled" while you are working the problem). Does knowing the correct answer make you want to check or redo anything? Go ahead.

Finally, work your way through the official solution—but stop whenever you get a good idea about anything. See how far you can push that idea yourself before you continue reading the official solution. Make yourself work for it! You'll learn better that way.

Step 1: Understand the Prompt and Question

The accompanying blurb explains that the table provides total and percent of sales numbers across six months. It also explains why the Automotive division seemingly had no sales in January and February: because that division was acquired in March.

The Total column shows a significant jump in March, corresponding with the acquisition of the new division. Other than that, sales are generally increasing, though May shows a drop. The percentages for Electronics and Housewares drop in March, but this occurs because a third division is added; *sales in dollars* haven't necessarily dropped in the other two divisions, just their *share* of total sales.

This fact—that a new division was acquired partway through the period—means the data is going to be a little odd. Make a note to yourself to be especially careful with any questions that ask you to bridge the pre- and post-acquisition periods—perhaps jot down Feb and Mar on your scratch paper as your reminder. You may have to do some calculations in order to be able to compare the numbers in a meaningful way.

> For each of the following statements, select *Would help explain* if the statement would, if true, help explain some of the information in the table. Otherwise, select *Would not help explain*.

The *if true* language in the question stem sends a specific message: You are supposed to accept each statement as true. In other words, your job here is not to decide whether the statement is true. Rather, assuming already that the statement *is* true, does that statement help to explain some portion of the data that you see in the table?

This question is essentially the opposite of what you were asked to do on the last problem. You're not taking the table data and seeing whether you can prove that the statement is true. You're starting from the given statement and seeing whether it makes that data make sense.

Here's the first statement:

Would help explain	Would not help explain	
O	O	Consumer purchases of electronics typically drop just after the month of December, but they revive within two to three months.

Step 2: Plan Your Approach

Just after the month of December would be January, and January is included in the data. The statement is limited to the Electronics division.

Assume that this statement is true. If so, what would you expect to see in the data? It should be the case that January and possibly February Electronics revenues should be lower and then the numbers should increase possibly in February and certainly in March. Check the data to see whether this trend exists.

Ah, but the table doesn't show revenues just for the Electronics division. It shows total revenues and then the percentage of those revenues attributed to each division. So you are going to need to do some calculating to see what's happening with the revenues in this one division.

Step 3: Solve the Problem

From January to February, you have only the two data points (Electronics and Housewares), so you can eyeball the numbers. The Electronics percentage for February increased month-over-month, as did total sales, so Electronics purchases did go up from January to February. Did they go up in March as well?

In March, the Electronics percentage was 34.19%, or approximately $\frac{1}{3}$ of total revenues. Revenues were $6,561, or approximately $6,600, so a third is about $2,200. (Note: The revenues are in thousands in the table—that is, revenue was really about $6.561 million—but you can ignore that detail when you're just trying to figure out whether revenue increased or decreased.)

Total revenues in February were about $4,200 and Electronics represented 49.75% of that, or about 50%. So February revenues were about $2,100.

If you feel that the numbers are so close ($2,100 and $2,200) that your estimations could be in error, pop up the calculator and calculate the figure for which you had to estimate more heavily—in this case, March. Jot down the calculation first on your scrap paper: (6,600)(0.3419). The value is $2,243 (and change), so yes, it is the case that revenue increased in March.

Overall, revenue went up both from January to February and from February to March.

For March to April, you now have all three divisions in the mix, so you can eyeball again. Electronics increased its percentage share *and* total revenues increased, so Electronics went up yet again in this period.

This statement does explain what's happening with the data for the Electronics division. The correct answer for statement 1 is *Would help explain*.

Repeat the UPS steps as you work through the second and third statements. Here's the second statement:

Would help explain	Would not help explain	
○	○	Companies that have electronics, housewares, and automotive product lines tend to have higher total sales in housewares than do companies that sell only one or two of these product lines.

Hmm. If a company sells all three lines, then it tends to sell more in housewares than does a company with only one or two of these lines. This prompt is only about one company, though, so how can you tell anything about a company that sells only one or two of these product lines?

Wait! For the first two months of the period shown in the table, this company did sell only two of these product lines. So compare the company to itself, pre- and post-acquisition.

In this case, it isn't necessary to sort the data at all, but you will have to do a little number crunching:

Month	Total ($, thousands)	% Electronics	% Housewares	% Automotive
January	3,890	47.09	52.91	0.00
February	4,204	49.75	50.25	0.00
March	6,561	34.19	33.00	32.81
April	6,982	36.44	34.03	29.53
May	6,613	37.97	33.34	28.69
June	7,028	34.58	34.00	31.42

In February, Housewares had about 50% of sales, or about $2,100 (you can continue to ignore the *thousands* designation). It had a slightly higher percentage share in January, but total sales were $300 lower that month, so the dollar amount for Housewares in January was lower than in February.

In March, the automotive business was acquired. Now, Housewares dropped to 33% of total sales, but of a larger base: $6,561. Approximately one-third of that figure is about $2,200, so Housewares sales did grow from February to March.

In April, Housewares increased its share of sales and total revenues increased, so housewares was again greater in April than in February. Likewise, in both May and June, Housewares had a greater share than in March and total revenues were greater than in March, so the trend continues.

The correct answer for statement 2 is *Would help explain*.

Here's the third statement:

Would help explain	Would not help explain	
O	O	The Housewares division took a $1.1 million loss in March due to an accounting change.

Don't jump straight to the data and start calculating anything. Understand first. This statement talks about a loss, but the data in the table is entirely about revenues. A loss is a cost; it would be reflected in profits, not in revenues. So the data in the table can't help to explain this cost.

Note: The GMAT doesn't expect you to know about accounting—you'll learn that in grad school!—but it does expect you to know that Profit = Revenue − Cost.

The correct answer for statement 3 is *Would not help explain*.

The answers are:

Would help explain	Would not help explain	
●	○	Consumer purchases of electronics typically drop just after the month of December, but they revive within two to three months.
●	○	Companies that have electronics, housewares, and automotive product lines tend to have higher total sales in housewares than do companies that sell only one or two of these product lines.
○	●	The Housewares division took a $1.1 million loss in March due to an accounting change.

If you made a mistake at any step along the way, first try to isolate the error. If you fell into a trap because of the confusing data switch in March, when the Automotive division was acquired, the unusual data there was your clue to pause for a moment. The two 0.0% entries really stand out; something weird happened. Try to understand what happened and why before you get to the statements.

Note that when a table adds a set of data partway through, you can't compare the data sets as easily, particularly when the percentages have to add up to 100% (as in this case). Expect at least one of the statements to hinge on that change, and be prepared to do a little number crunching.

In this case, you had to deal with that change in multiple statements; in fact, that was the main focus of most of the problem. You didn't even have to sort on this table.

Don't hesitate to pop up the on-screen calculator when you need it—just make sure that you know what you need to calculate before you start punching numbers. Also, you can estimate a lot of the time; for example, 50.25% is close enough to 50% to estimate, and then you don't need to pull up the calculator at all.

Practice Your Skills

You're ready to practice and get better at Tables! Because most IR problems have some amount of interactivity (e.g., you need to sort on Table problems), your practice problems are located online in your Atlas study center. If you have access to Manhattan Prep's *GMAT All the Quant* guide, you may want to review the chapter on Statistics before doing more Table problems.

Graphics Interpretation

In This Chapter

- UPS for Graphs

- Types of Graphs

- Review and Improve on Nonstandard Graphs

- Review and Improve on Standard Graphs

In this chapter, you will learn about the types of standard and not-so-standard graphs that can appear on the exams, and you'll learn how to apply the Understand–Plan–Solve (UPS) process to all Graph problems.

CHAPTER 5 Graphics Interpretation

Graphics Interpretation (Graph) problems can be built on a wide variety of types of graphs, charts, and diagrams, even non-math-based ones. You'll see many examples in this chapter, particularly of the "traditional" types of math graphs.

(Note: In the real world of data analysis, graphs and charts are not quite the same thing. But for the purposes of the exam, you can use these two terms interchangeably.)

Graph prompts consist of some sort of graphic with some accompanying text. The question always has two parts and always appears below the graph prompt. The example below shows a traditional type of math graph: a scatterplot:

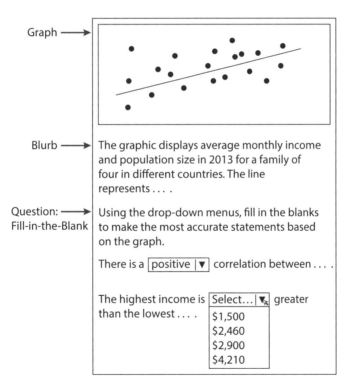

Many graphs are common types that you've seen before: pie charts, bar charts, line graphs, and the like. The exam will expect you to know how to read these already; you'll learn how in this chapter. Other types could include Venn diagrams, timelines, organizational hierarchies, even geometry diagrams. If you are given a graph that doesn't fall into a standard math categorization, don't worry; you'll always be given instructions regarding what it is and how to read it.

The question consists of one or two sentences with two blanks. Your task is to fill in each blank with the best answer, chosen from a drop-down menu sitting right there in the blank. You'll have three to five answer choices for any one blank.

As on other Integrated Reasoning question types, this is considered a single multipart question, so you have to answer both parts correctly in order to earn credit for the problem.

The two blanks may be related to each other, in which case you'll need to solve both simultaneously. The two blanks may also be completely separate from each other.

UPS for Graphs

As discussed in the Introduction to Integrated Reasoning chapter, you'll use the UPS process to solve all IR problems, including Graphs. UPS stands for Understand the prompt and question, Plan, and Solve.

Graph questions most often have a quantitative focus, often testing general Statistics (mean, median, standard deviation, range, correlation, and so on) Fractions, Decimals, Percents, and Ratios. Some questions, though, are not quant-focused and instead revolve around your ability to figure out how to read the graph or diagram and think logically about the information presented.

Step 1: Understand the Prompt and Question

Take a look at this Graph prompt:

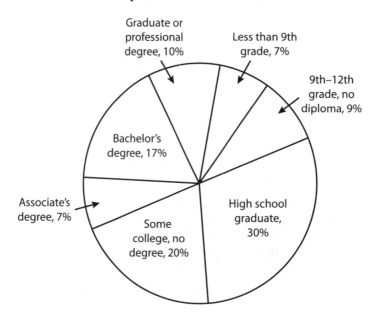

2013 Population 25 Years and Over

In 2013, the percent of the population aged 25 years and over that did NOT have a bachelor's, graduate, or professional degree is [Select... |▾]

Select...
7%
16%
27%
59%
73%

(Note: Unlike this example, an official question will always have two blanks, each with its own set of options.)

What jumps out?

First, at a glance, this is a pie chart, one of the common types of math graphs. But don't start to look at the data yet. You have one other thing to do first.

As on Table problems, use SEE, with one slight change. This time, SEE stands for Select, Eyeball, and Estimate. On the actual test, you will see a box in each blank with the word *Select* and a little drop-down icon. Click on the word *Select* to glance at the multiple-choice options for that blank.

The form of the answers can completely change how you decide to approach a problem, so you want to glance at the answers very early in the process. In fact, glance at those answers right now. Notice anything?

The answers are in percent form, so math is involved. They are also spread pretty far apart. That's a clue that you may be able to estimate to solve. Now you know to examine the possibilities for estimation as you orient yourself to the prompt.

Now, go back to the graph. Read the title and any accompanying text in order to understand what the graph is all about. In this case, the title indicates that the chart provides information about a certain population in a certain year.

Next, dive into the graph itself. The wedges are labeled by type of schooling and show a percentage for each, but no real numbers. Since this is a pie chart, the percentages add up to 100%. (You don't need to check this. This is true for all pie charts.)

The answer choices are also in the form of percents, so you might need to add up some of the categories of the pie chart or maybe multiply some things together. The calculations could be tedious, but the answer choices are pretty spread apart, so you can estimate fairly aggressively. With luck, you won't even have to pull up the calculator.

Before you start to read the sentence, click on the first drop-down menu so that the multiple-choice options appear. Read the sentence with these options showing. (For a real question, which has two drop-downs, click on the second drop-down menu after you get past the part of the sentence that has the first blank.)

The question asks about certain categories of people: those with a bachelor's, graduate, or professional degree. Take careful note of that capitalized word NOT; the question is actually asking you to find the percentage of all others, *not* those three. You might even jot down that word.

Jotting down important information helps you to fix that information in your brain. You'll be less likely to forget or to make a careless mistake.

Step 2: Plan Your Approach

Given that there are five categories in the "wanted" group and only two in the "not wanted" group, it will be more efficient to add up the two "not wanted" categories and subtract from 100% in order to find the sum of the remaining five groups. That represents fewer math steps than adding up five numbers.

One more thing: The most common error is probably going to be that someone misses the word NOT and so solves for the "not wanted" group by accident. Expect to see that trap among the list of answers.

Further, since these two groups have to add up to 100%, if you have to guess, choose an answer that is part of a pair that adds to 100%. (In fact, only one pair of numbers fits this pattern: 27% and 73%.)

Step 3: Solve the Problem

Find the percentage for the two unwanted categories, bachelor's degree and graduate or professional degree:

$$17\% + 10\% = 27\%$$

Bingo! That's the "not wanted" group and that (trap) value is in the answers. Don't pick it. The correct answer is the other one in the pair, 73%.

In this case, it's not all that hard to add up the two numbers, 17 and 10. On another problem, with more cumbersome numbers, you could estimate at this stage, since the answers are pretty far apart.

Types of Graphs

Some graphs will be very familiar to you; others may seem unusual. You've probably seen a number of pie charts and bar graphs in your life, and you'll see these on Integrated Reasoning questions as well. On the other end of the spectrum, you might see a diagram that was completely made up for this test.

Here are some examples of more standard diagrams:

Column

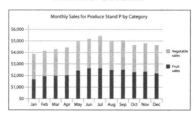

Stacked Column

Clustered Column

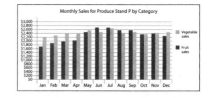

Bar

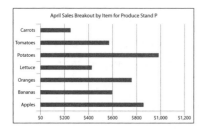

Line

Scatterplot

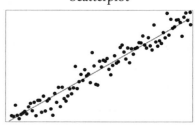

Pie Chart

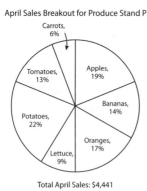

Bubble Chart

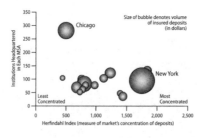

Venn Diagram

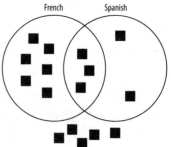

Organizational Chart Timeline Others are possible!

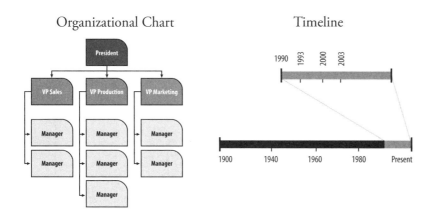

Don't let all these columns, lines, and shapes scare you. These display formats are commonly used in business and academic settings today—and you've seen most, if not all, of the math-based ones before. When the exam does give a nonstandard visual, it will be the kind of diagram you might see in a company presentation, an annual report, or a business-school case study. You'll be given some kind of context to help you understand it.

The following are the most common types of standard math graphs that you're likely to see on the exam. As you review them, test yourself: See what you notice about a given chart before you read the chapter text explaining how that type of chart works. What kind of information can you glean? And what kind of analyses can you make?

Column and Bar Charts

A column chart shows amounts as heights, so you would scan for changes in the heights as you move from left to right. For example:

Column chart: Scan left to right.

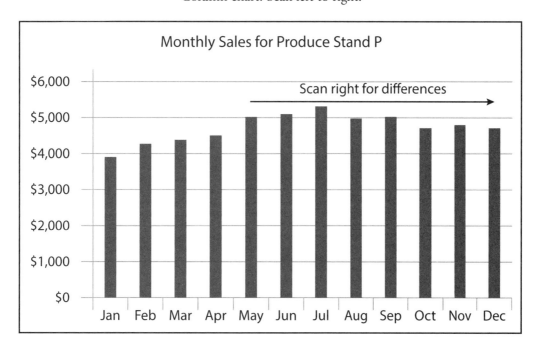

Similarly, bar charts show amounts as lengths, so you would scan for differences in those lengths as you move from top to bottom. For example:

Bar chart: Scan top to bottom.

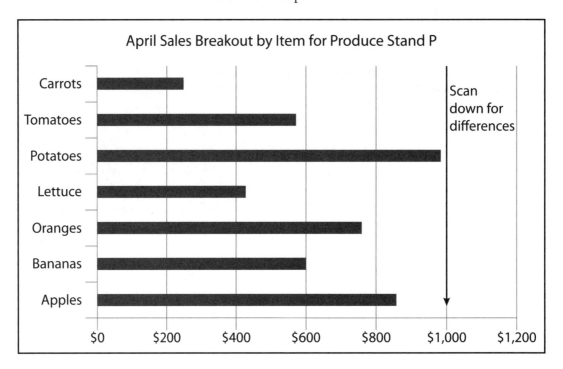

Column charts are often used to show trends over time, while bar charts are more frequently used for non-time comparisons (e.g., carrots vs. apples).

It can be difficult to read a value from a column or bar that ends *between* grid lines. The grid lines are those lighter grey lines that divide the graph into sections—for example, in the column chart, the grid lines show up at $1,000, $2,000, and so on up to $6,000.

If the column or bar does not end exactly on a grid line, you're going to have to estimate a little. Hold your finger, your pen, or even the edge of your scratch paper up to the screen to make a straight line, and take your best guess. (This will be close enough—don't worry!)

A question might ask you to calculate the percent increase or decrease from one time period to the next. Consider the Monthly Sales column graph given earlier, and answer the following:

What was the approximate percent increase in sales from April to May?

Estimate April sales to be $4,500 (the column ends about halfway between $4,000 and $5,000). May's column ends right on $5,000. Now use the percent change formula:

$$\frac{\text{May sales} - \text{April sales}}{\text{April sales}} \approx \frac{5,000 - 4,500}{4,500} = \frac{1}{9} \approx 11\%$$

Variations on Column and Bar Charts

If there is more than one series of numbers, the exam might use a stacked or clustered column chart. The stacked form places the two data points in the same column, one on top of the other, so it emphasizes the *sum* of the two series of numbers. For example:

Stacked column: Emphasizes *sums*.

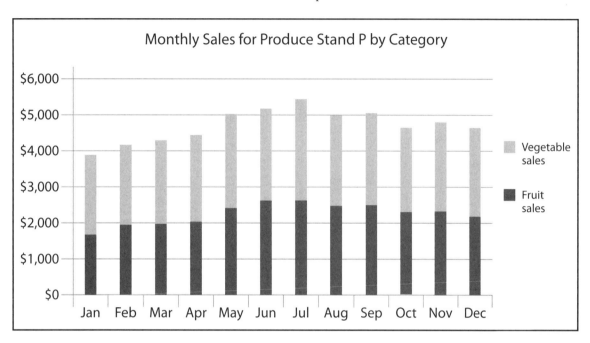

Note that, in the stacked column graph, it's easy to find the values for fruit sales and for total sales (fruit and vegetable together), but it's not easy to see the values for vegetable sales. You could use subtraction to find the value—for example, in January, vegetable sales were about $3,800 − $1,700 = $2,100.

You could also, though, eyeball by using the grid lines. The difference between any one set of grid lines is $1,000; call this one "segment" of the graph. Mentally take the entire lighter grey part of the column for January and move it up a little bit so that it starts right on the $2,000 grid line. (You can use your fingers to help eyeball this on the test screen.)

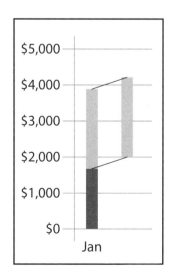

The lighter grey part of the column covers a little bit more than two segments of the graph, so the value is a little more than $2,000, or about $2,100.

The clustered column graph, by contrast, highlights which of the two values is greater at any point along the way. For example:

Clustered column: Emphasizes *differences*.

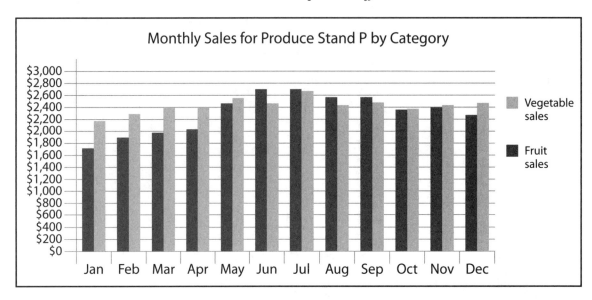

Now, finding the values for each individual category is straightforward, but you would have to add up the two paired columns to find the total sales for that month.

You might think that, if the test wants you to work with the total, it will give you the stacked column, since that shows the total—but not necessarily. And the test writers are not just being deliberately unhelpful to irritate you! The test wants to make sure that you know how to use the kinds of graphs you're likely to need to use in grad school, and you will often want to figure things out that don't fit perfectly with the type of graph given. They really are testing real-world skills with these problems.

Line Charts

Line charts are very similar to column charts. However, each number is shown as a floating dot rather than as a column, and the dots are connected by lines. The *x*-axis almost always represents time, since the lines imply connection. Although lines are continuous, do *not* assume that the data is itself continuous. If it is monthly data, for example, then the chart is showing just that one monthly data point—the line connecting one month to the next does not represent day-by-day data. For example:

Line

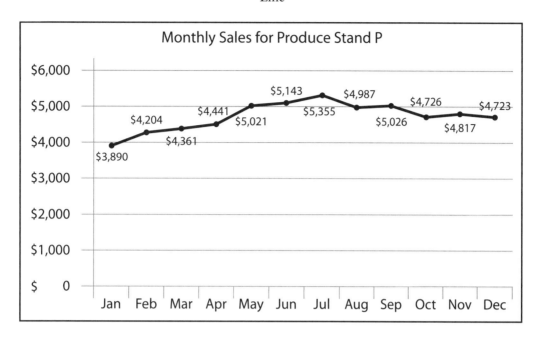

You could also have a line chart that contains multiple lines. Multiple lines are used to show multiple data series changing over time. When the desired emphasis is on the change within each set over time, this graph is more clear than a clustered column graph. For example:

Line (with two data series)

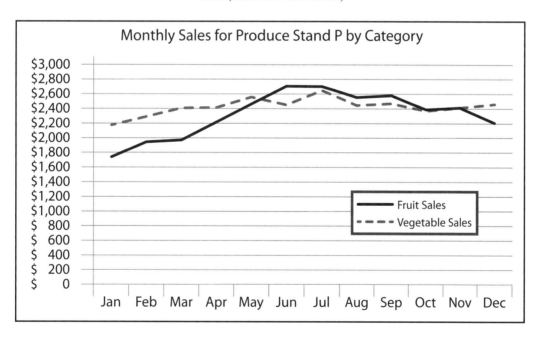

Compare this to the clustered column chart shown earlier. Both charts show how fruit sales compare to vegetable sales in any given month. Here, though, it's easier to see that fruit sales peak in the June–July time frame but are at their lowest in January, while vegetable sales are more steady throughout the year.

Scatterplots

A scatterplot is a more complex graph. It shows the relationship between two columns of data in a table. Each point on the plot represents a single record (a single row). For example:

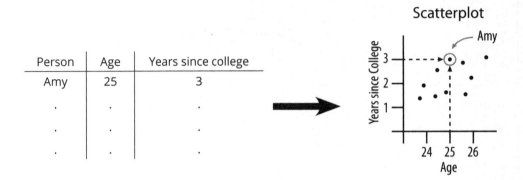

The overall pattern of the dots indicates how the two columns of numbers vary together, if at all. For example, glance back at the very first sample Graph problem shown at the beginning of this chapter. It shows a scatterplot. As you move to the right on the *x*-axis, the dots also tend to move up on the *y*-axis. In other words, as the *x* value increases, the *y* value also tends to increase.

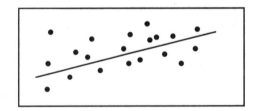

The graph above is showing a correlation between the two sets of data points—in this case, a positive correlation. If you draw a line showing the general trend of the points (as shown in the graphic), the line slopes upward from left to right.

If this sounds familiar, that's because you first learned about this in the Table chapter. Feel free to jump back there right now and remind yourself of what you learned. These kinds of callbacks are great for helping people to remember and recall the information they've learned.

A graph can also show a negative correlation: As one set of data points increases, the other set decreases. If you drew a trend line on such a graph, that line would slope downward from left to right.

If there's no trend—that is, sometimes the points go up and sometimes they go down, with no real connection—then the data in that graph has no correlation at all.

Pie Charts

A pie chart is used to show the relative sizes of "slices" as proportions of a whole, so pie charts are typically used when the test writers want to ask you about percents. The size of the angle of the pie slice is proportional to that item's percent of the whole, and all of the pieces of the pie add up to 100%.

Sometimes the pie chart shows real amounts and sometimes it directly shows percents, but even when there are real numbers, you will probably have to calculate something in terms of a percent. Percents on various slices will always be a percent of the whole.

Take a look at this example:

Pie

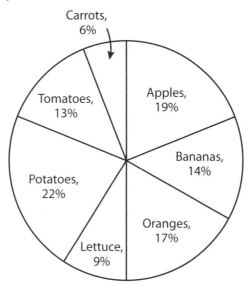

April Sales Breakout for Produce Stand P

Total April Sales: $4,441

Since the total April sales figure is given ($4,441), you can calculate the dollar sales of any item, or any group of items, in the pie.

Try this problem:

> What is the total dollar value of lettuce and tomato sales for Produce Stand P in April?

Take a look at the following two sets of answers. How are they different? How might you approach the problem differently, depending on which set of answers you were actually given?

Set 1	Set 2
$103.52	$797.64
$514.91	$895.43
$977.02	$977.02
$1,348.37	$1,120.51

How would that change how you decide to solve?

In the first set, the answers are spread quite far apart, so you can estimate aggressively.

Lettuce and tomato sales are equal to 9% plus 13%, which sums to 22%, or about 20%.

You can take 20% of $4,400 (the approximate April sales) with a minimum of effort. First, take 10% by moving the decimal to the left one place. Then, multiply that number by 2 to get 20%:

$$20\% \times 4,400 = 440 \times 2 = 880$$

Is that close enough? Glance at the first set of answers. The calculation underestimated a bit, so the correct answer must be larger, and the only one that's close enough is $977.02.

That estimation is not quite good enough for the second set of answers, though, so make the calculation just a little more precise. You've already found 20%. Use that to find 2% and then add to get 22%:

$$
\begin{aligned}
20\% \times 4,400 &= 440 \times 2 = 880 \\
2\% \times 4,400 &= 44 \times 2 = 88 \\
\hline
22\% & = 968
\end{aligned}
$$

Lettuce and tomato sales are approximately $968, so the correct answer is $977.02.

Note that you *under*estimated the starting number in the calculation. The value you calculate, therefore, will be too small but close enough.

If you don't spot the 22% shortcut—or if the numbers you're working with don't allow you to use that shortcut—you can try one other way. The first time, you underestimated a bit and got $880. Next, overestimate a bit: Find 25% of $4,400.

The fastest way to find 25% of a figure is to divide by 4 (or to divide by 2 twice). In this case, $4,400 divided by 4 is $1,100. This is an overestimation, so that last answer choice is too big. Only $977.02 works.

By the way, a pie chart can show only one series of data. If you see two pie charts, they represent two separate series of data.

Other Types of Charts

The test writers can draw any kind of diagram or visual they want. Don't panic. Read the title, read the labels, and try to understand how the graph is laid out visually. If you're stuck, focus on just one small part, such as a single data point. What does that point represent? What do you know about that piece of data? Then, work your way out from there.

(Or not! You will want to guess immediately on several Integrated Reasoning questions overall. If you see a graph that just doesn't make any sense, make this problem one of your guesses.)

Bubble charts look intimidating, but they are just scatterplots on steroids. Rather than two pieces of information about each point, you have three. In order to show that third dimension, all the little points are expanded to varying sizes—and those varying sizes give you a relative measure of that third dimension. For example:

Bubble

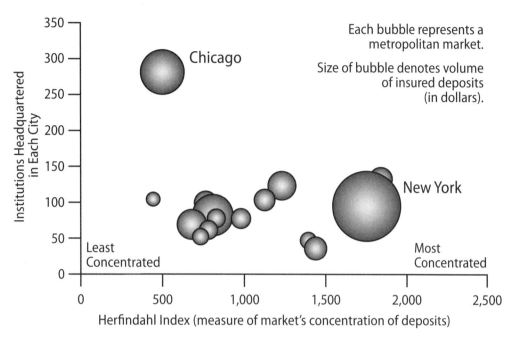

Bank Deposit Concentration in Large Metropolitan Statistical Areas

Sources: Summary of Deposits, June 2002; FDIC's Research and Information System, June 30, 2003.
Note: Fifteen largest markets shown, based on number of institutions headquartered there.

There are two really big bubbles labeled with city names, so compare them. New York has a bigger bubble than Chicago. What does that bubble represent? The *volume of insured deposits*. So more insured deposits are made in New York than in Chicago. (Not sure what insured deposits are? Don't worry about it—right now, it's enough to know that New York has more than Chicago does of whatever this thing is.)

The Chicago bubble is higher up the *y*-axis than the New York bubble. What does that mean? Look at the *y*-axis label: More companies of a certain type (banks in this case) are headquartered in Chicago. That's interesting.

Finally, the New York bubble is farther to the right along the *x*-axis. What does that mean? The *Herfindahl Index* is weird but the chart itself shows the text *Least Concentrated* and *Most Concentrated* at either end of the *x*-axis. So New York is more concentrated than Chicago—whatever *more concentrated* means.

You may only need to understand that New York has this characteristic, not what the label truly means, so don't spend any time now trying to "really" understand. Look at the question first and then decide what you need to try to understand more fully.

Speaking of the question, try this:

> There is _____ correlation between the value of insured deposits and the Herfindahl Index.

(A) a positive

(B) a negative

(C) no

The question specifies two of the three dimensions: the Herfindahl Index (position along the *x*-axis) and the value of insured deposits (the size of the bubbles). A positive correlation would mean that the bubbles tend to increase in size the farther right you go on the *x*-axis. Is this the case?

Not really. The largest bubble is far to the right, but the next largest one is far to the left, as is the third largest and possibly the fourth or fifth largest.

Is this a negative correlation, then? In this case, the bubbles would be larger to the left and generally decrease as you move to the right—but the placement of New York absolutely kills this possibility.

The correct answer is *no* correlation. There isn't a consistent trend, or connection, between the placement of the bubble along the *x*-axis and the size of the bubble.

What else can the exam throw at you? You may have run across Venn diagrams during your study for the Quant portion of the exam. Venn diagrams consist of two (or three) overlapping circles, showing how two (or three) groups overlap. Here's a two-circle example showing the number of students in certain classes:

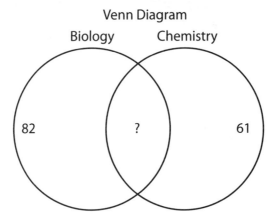

This Venn diagram indicates that there are 82 people in the biology-only group and 61 in the chemistry-only group, as well as an unknown number in the overlap between the two groups. The diagram would be accompanied by a blurb providing additional information, possibly asking you to calculate the number of people in both groups (or in neither group).

The organizational (org) chart and the expanded timeline shown below are good examples of non-math graphs. (Timelines don't have to run horizontally, by the way!)

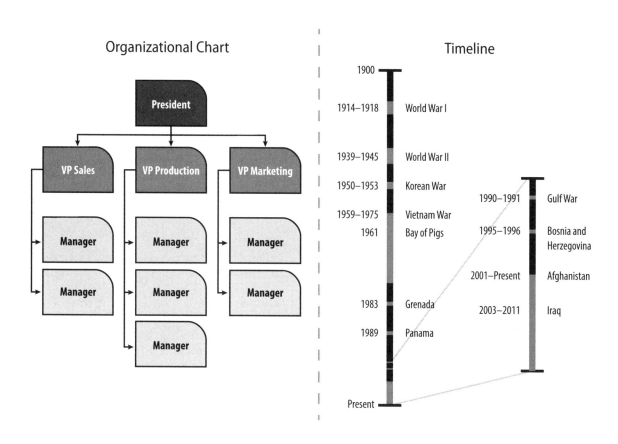

Typical org charts show hierarchical relationships within a business. Expanded timelines give you both a big picture of events in order and a "zoomed in" look at one part of the picture. Note that the scales in the different sections are different; be ready to make comparisons across those different scales.

Here are some other examples of nonstandard graphs, just to give you an idea:

- A diagram showing the workflow or set of steps a company uses to make a certain product
- A genealogy tree or other diagram to show inherited genetic traits or shared characteristics from one generation to the next
- A map showing data tied to different geographical regions
- A project schedule or timeline, possibly showing dependencies across different steps of the project

Anything is possible—which sounds more unsettling than it is. First, most of the nonstandard charts you see will specifically be designed to be read and used intuitively. After all, in the real world, poorly designed charts are rarely adopted for widespread use. Second, you will be given some direction in the blurb as to how to read the visual. Use the blurb to help you interpret the diagram.

Review and Improve on Nonstandard Graphs

Try out another problem, this time with a nonstandard graph:

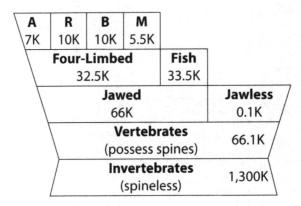

The diagram displays the number of living species represented by two nonoverlapping categories, Vertebrates and Invertebrates, which together comprise all animal species. The diagram also displays the various subcategories of Vertebrates and the approximate number of species in each (the abbreviation K stands for thousands). In the top row, A stands for amphibians, R stands for reptiles, B stands for birds, and M stands for mammals.

Based on the given information, use the drop-down menus to most accurately complete the following statements.

Four-limbed species represent approximately | Select... ▼ | of all vertebrate species. Amphibians

| 2.5% |
| 15% |
| 35% |
| 50% |

and reptiles combined comprise approximately | Select... ▼ | of all animal species.

$$\frac{1}{200}$$

$$\frac{1}{100}$$

$$\frac{1}{4}$$

$$\frac{1}{2}$$

How did it go? Before reading the explanation below (or even checking whether you got it right), review your work yourself. Is there anything you want to try calculating a different way? Do you want to double-check anything? Go for it.

Next, check just the correct answer. (Glance ahead. It's listed just before Step 1 of the walk-through.) Does knowing that give you any ideas for what to check or do a different way?

If you answered the question incorrectly—or aren't fully confident about something you answered correctly—review each step of the process thoroughly using the official solution. Did you overlook, misunderstand, or fail to comprehend any information in the prompt? Did you answer the question that was asked? Was there a better way to approach the problem? Did you make any mistakes at the solution stage?

If you answered the question correctly and were confident even before you saw the correct answer, then scan the walk-through below for any ideas about how to solve more efficiently. Are there any shortcuts or other methods you can use to make the job easier?

The correct answer for the first blank is fifty percent and the correct answer for the second blank is one one-hundredth. (These are written out in words so that you don't inadvertently spot the correct answers before you're ready to know!)

Step 1: Understand the Prompt and Question

The diagram is not a standard chart, so you will definitely use the blurb to help you understand it. Before doing that, though, take the first step in SEE: Click the *Select* drop-downs to see what the answers are. Both are math-focused. The answers for the first part of the question are in percentage form. They are far enough apart that you may be able to estimate at least enough to knock out some of the answers.

The answers for the second part of the question are in fraction form. The first two are clustered together and the final two are clustered together, so you may be able to eyeball enough to narrow down to two answers— that's a valid strategy if it looks like it may take too long to fully solve.

Now, examine the text. The blurb first mentions *two nonoverlapping categories, Vertebrates and Invertebrates.* Glance at the diagram itself: These two categories appear at the bottom.

Nonoverlapping means that no animal appears in both categories. Further, the first sentence also states that these two categories *together comprise all animal species*, so all animals are either V or Inv. Abbreviate as you jot down this information.

The blurb further explains that the boxes above the V box represent *subcategories* of V and that the numbers represent *the number (in thousands) of species*. Glance at the diagram again.

V's are split into the categories Jawed or Jawless. Total, there are 66K V's, most of which are jawed. Only a very small number are jawless. The jawed vertebrates can then be broken down into the categories Four-Limbed or Fish, and there are roughly equal numbers of each. Finally, the Four-Limbed group can be broken into four subgroups whose names appear only in the blurb: amphibians, reptiles, birds, and mammals. Reptiles and birds are the largest categories and mammals are the smallest category.

The question consists of two separate sentences. The first asks you to find Four-Limbed as a percent of Vertebrate. The second wants to know what fraction A's and R's represent of all species.

The two parts are not related, so you'll solve each individually.

Step 2: Plan Your Approach

In each case, the task is to make sure that you are working with the right categories. (In general, if you see a nonstandard diagram that has a bunch of subcategories of subcategories, chances are good that at least part of your job will be to make sure you're working with the right categories.) Organize your work carefully and double-check, before calculating, that you have pulled the data from the right groups.

Finally, keep an eye on the answer choices as you go; don't do more math than you have to do.

Step 3: Solve the Problem

The first part asks for Four-Limbed as a percent of Vertebrates. The Four-Limbed category has about 32.5K members and the Vertebrate category has about 66K members. Half of 66 is 33, so four-limbed species represent approximately 50% of all vertebrate species.

The second part asks for amphibians and reptiles as a fraction of all animal species. Jot down A + R for the top of the fraction. What about the bottom? Is that all vertebrates? Look back at the prompt.

No, it's not just the vertebrates. The blurb says that vertebrates and invertebrates *together* make up all animal species, so you'll need to add V and Inv. (Just double-check first that they didn't already tell you the total in the prompt—but they didn't.)

$$\text{Total animals} = 1{,}300\text{K} + 66\text{K} = 1{,}366\text{K}$$

That's the bottom of the fraction. What goes on top?

$$\text{A} + \text{R} = 7\text{K} + 10\text{K} = 17\text{K}$$

Here's the full fraction:

$$\frac{17}{1{,}366}$$

Hmm. That's much smaller than $\frac{1}{2}$ or $\frac{1}{4}$, so eliminate those two answers. But which of the other answers is it? One way to find out: Plug that fraction into the calculator. The decimal is 0.0124. The decimal value of $\frac{1}{100}$ is 0.01, and the decimal value of $\frac{1}{200}$ is 0.02. The value 0.0124 is closer to 0.01, so the correct answer is $\frac{1}{100}$.

If you're not a fan of decimals, you can also simplify the fraction. The problem tells you that you can estimate and the two remaining answers are quite far apart, so you can estimate aggressively:

$$\frac{17}{1{,}366} = \frac{20}{1{,}400} = \frac{1}{70}$$

That fraction is closer to $\frac{1}{100}$, so that's the correct answer.

Here's one more way! Work backwards from the two remaining answers. If $\frac{1}{100}$ is the correct answer, then that fraction would approximately equal $\frac{17}{1{,}366}$. Does it? Use your calculator to find out (and do the same for the other remaining answer):

$$\text{Is } \frac{1}{100} \approx \frac{17}{1{,}366} \text{ ?} \qquad\qquad \text{Is } \frac{1}{200} \approx \frac{17}{1{,}366} \text{ ?}$$

$$\text{Is } 1{,}366\left(\frac{1}{100}\right) \approx 17 \text{ ?} \qquad \text{Is } 1{,}366\left(\frac{1}{200}\right) \approx 17 \text{ ?}$$

$$\text{Is } 14 \approx 17 \text{ ?} \qquad\qquad\qquad \text{Is } 7 \approx 17 \text{ ?}$$

The fraction $\frac{1}{100}$ is a closer match.

Therefore, four-limbed species represent approximately $\boxed{50\%}$ of all vertebrate species. Amphibians and reptiles combined comprise approximately $\boxed{\dfrac{1}{100}}$ of all animal species.

Review and Improve on Standard Graphs

Try the process one more time:

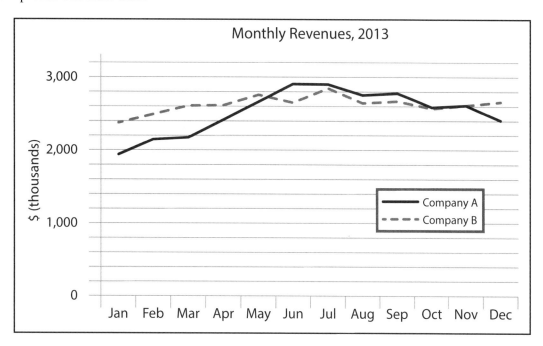

The chart shows 2013 monthly revenues reported by Company A and Company B, which compete in the cellphone market.

Based on the given information, use the drop-down menus to most accurately complete the following statement:

In 2013, Company A's annual revenues were [Select... | ▼]. Company B's annual revenues and the

>
<
=

positive difference between the two figures was approximately [Select... | ▼].

0
250,000
750,000
1,250,000
3,000,000

How did it go? For your review, follow the same steps introduced for the problem about the Vertebrates and Invertebrates. First, take stock. How did you feel about the whole thing? Anything you want to try again?

Next, check just the correct answer. (It's at the very end of the explanation.) Does knowing that give you any ideas for what to check or do a different way?

Whether you answered the problem correctly or incorrectly, review each step of the process. Look for ways to do the problem better or faster next time, and look for clues to tell you when to guess and move on.

Step 1: Understand the Prompt and Question

This is a line chart. The first set of answers requires you only to be able to tell whether one thing is greater than, less than, or equal to something else; there's a good chance you'll be able to eyeball this. The second blank requires a real value, but the answer choices are far enough apart that you'll likely be able to estimate.

Also note that the answers for the second blank seem way too big compared to the *y*-axis given in the graph. The graph is in thousands as shown by the *y*-axis label. The answers show the real number, not the abbreviated numbers shown on the graph.

Use that as your segue into the chart itself. It shows monthly revenues in thousands of dollars during 2013 for two different companies. For example, a point at 2,000 indicates revenues of $2,000,000, or $2 million.

This is a line graph, so you may need to determine differences between points on the line. That's easiest to do by counting segments of the graph, so figure out what each horizontal line segment represents and jot down that figure. In this case, each segment represents 200, or $200,000.

In some months, Company A earned higher revenues; in other months, Company B did. Interestingly, Company B started higher and finished higher, while A jumped above B only in the middle of the year.

The two parts of the question ask for related information: which company had higher annual revenues and what that difference was. When this is the case, think about how to save yourself some time and effort by solving the statements simultaneously.

Step 2: Plan Your Approach

The first part asks whether Company A's revenues were greater, less than, or equal to Company B's, so plan to track the difference in terms of Company A.

The standard math way to solve would be to mark down every monthly figure and add them all up for both companies, then compare the two figures. That involves adding 24 numbers, though—way too much work! There has to be an easier way.

There is! Count only the differences between the figures. Further, use the segments to make your calculations easier. Count just by segments, then multiply by 200 (the value of one segment) to convert to the actual figure.

Finally, don't worry about the *thousands of dollars* part of things for now; solve using the *y*-axis scale and add in three zeros later.

Step 3: Solve the Problem

First, just eyeball the graph. For the first five months, Company A is significantly below Company B, enough to create quite a large negative differential. Company B does lose some ground in the middle of the chart, but not enough to offset the initial differential, especially considering that Company B rebounds at the end of the year.

So Company A should end up lower than Company B. You'll have to calculate more precisely to know how much, but expect the answer to the first blank to be *less than*.

In January, Company A is about two segments below Company B. For this month, the differential is −2. The February differential is −1.5, so the total differential is now −3.5. Continue counting:

	Jan	Feb	Mar	Apr	May	Jun	Jul	Aug	Sep	Oct	Nov	Dec
Diff	−2	−1.5	−2	−1	−0.5	1	0	0.5	0.5	0	0	−1
Total	−2	−3.5	−5.5	−6.5	−7	−6	−6	−5.5	−5	−5	−5	−6

Company A finishes the year with −6 segments, which translates to a total of $(-6) \times (200) = -1{,}200$ below Company B. Add in three zeros, and Company A's revenue is $1,200,000 below Company B's.

Thus, in 2013, Company A's annual revenues were $\boxed{<}$ Company B's annual revenues, and the positive difference between the two figures was approximately $\boxed{1{,}250{,}000}$.

Counting by segments is a bit strange at first, but it saves a lot of time. Practice until you feel comfortable working with the numbers in this way. You don't actually need to make a table and write everything down. If you feel comfortable counting on screen, you can. Use a finger to point to each month's data as you solve, and consider jotting down just the total at the end of each month so that, if you lose track, you can check your work without having to start from the beginning.

You can also go the long way: Pull up the calculator and plug in each actual value to find the sums for each company. Only do this, though, if you have plenty of time. Don't sacrifice other questions later in the section because you spent too much time adding up 24 numbers at this stage.

If you think the second part will take too long to solve and you're not willing to make that investment, you can invest a small amount of time to increase your odds in making a guess. If you eyeball the data, you can tell that the first part is *less than* without calculating anything. That's also enough information to know that the answer to the second part is not going to be 0. Then, guess from here; you would have at least a 25% chance of guessing correctly.

Practice Your Skills

If you have access to Manhattan Prep's *GMAT All the Quant* guide, your next task is to study the unit on Fractions, Decimals, Percents, and Ratios, as well as the chapter on Statistics. As you become more conversant with these topics, you can practice more Graph problems in your Atlas online syllabus.

Multi-Source Reasoning

In This Chapter

- UPS for MSR

- Review and Improve on MSR

In this chapter, you will learn how to map the information from Multi-Source Reasoning (MSR) problems, as well as how to use Understand–Plan–Solve to approach the two types of questions that come with this problem type.

CHAPTER 6 Multi-Source Reasoning

Multi-Source Reasoning (MSR) problems are similar to Reading Comprehension (RC) passages, with two key differences: MSR can include mathematical data, graphics, and tables along with the text, and the information provided will be split across two or three tabs. Note: If you see a table in an MSR tab, you will *not* be able to sort the table.

Much like RC passages, the MSR prompts appear on the left side of the screen and the (typically) three accompanying questions appear on the right side of the screen, one at a time. These questions are of two different types: standard multiple-choice and either-or.

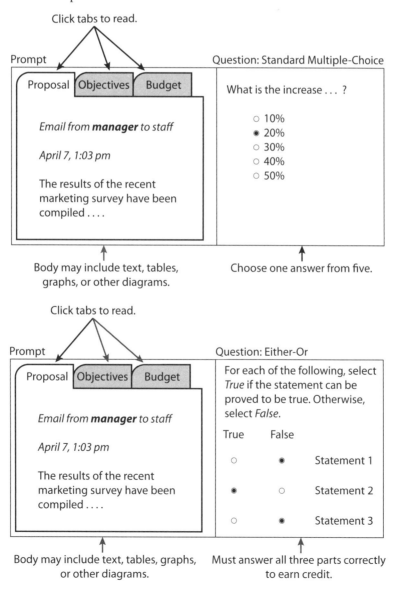

The most typical configuration for MSRs is one standard multiple-choice question and two separate either-or questions with three statements each. Occasionally, you might be given only two questions overall; more rarely, you might see four total questions.

The either-or questions will be in the same format that you've already seen on Table problems, and you can use the same techniques to solve.

The standard multiple-choice questions will be in the same format as problems in the Quant or Verbal sections of the exam, and you can often use the same techniques to solve. On a math-focused problem, you may be able to use smart numbers or work backwards. On a verbal-focused problem, you may be able to predict an answer (as on RC) or eliminate answers based on common traps that you've learned about for RC or Critical Reasoning.

As the word *multi-source* implies, the vast majority of questions will require you to integrate information from two or even all three of the tabs.

UPS for MSR

As with all Integrated Reasoning question types, you'll use the UPS process (Understand–Plan–Solve) to tackle MSR problems. Since there's quite a lot of information in the tabs, the Understand step is going to take some time. Because you will usually see three separate questions associated with the same MSR tabs, you can invest several minutes at the beginning to understand all of the information.

Step 1: Understand the Prompt and Question

Take a look at the two-tab MSR prompt below. Here's the first tab:

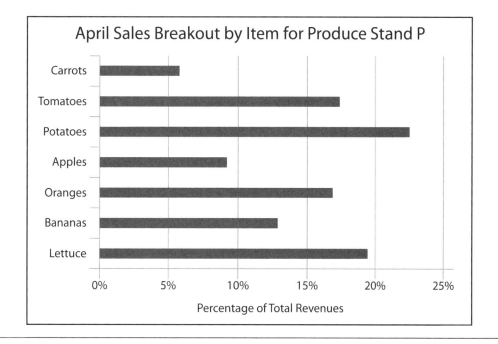

| Sales Breakout | Vitamin Content |

E-mail from Purchasing Supervisor to Sales Manager:

Total April sales for your produce stand were $4,441; the itemized data is below.

We already know that customers base their purchasing decisions on whether something is in season and how much it costs. Management believes that customers also care about the health factor, such as how high the vitamin content is for different types of produce. Do you have any data that could help us to evaluate this question?

We also need to think about pricing strategies in light of the fact that some items have a far longer shelf life. Potatoes will last weeks in cold storage, while the tomatoes won't last more than a few days without suffering a reduction in quality. Please send me any information you have about spoilage rates or other factors we should consider when setting prices.

Glance first at the labels on the two tabs: *Sales Breakout* and *Vitamin Content*. You might also choose to click briefly on the second tab to see whether it's pure text or whether it also contains a graph, table, or other non-text information. Don't read anything; just glance. (In this case, you'd see some text and a table—more on this in a bit.)

Now, go back to the first tab and start reading. Think about the "So what?" Why is the blurb telling you this? The blurb first sets some context and provides overall sales figures for a produce stand. The first big paragraph then talks about the factors that customers consider when buying produce and asks an explicit question about vitamin content. The second tab's title is actually *Vitamin Content*, so presumably that tab will address this question.

The second big paragraph raises the issue of shelf life for their pricing strategy. Perhaps the supervisor is thinking that they will have to reduce prices on certain items with a shorter shelf life in order to make sure they sell before they spoil. (She doesn't actually say this, but go ahead and speculate a little. Put yourself in the story.) The text also mentions spoilage rates, so perhaps the second tab will address this as well.

Finally, the bar graph provides the percentage of sales by item; there may be some calculations coming soon.

As you understand what's going on, jot down information on your scrap paper, but as with RC, don't take very detailed notes. The test is open book; the source information will be in front of you the whole time. Rather, you are going to create a **Tab Map** that will help you figure out where to go in order to answer the various questions.

All of the thoughts above might condense down into this map:

> #1 Sales
>
>   Apr $4,441
>
>   Buy in season. Cost. Care about V?
>
>   Pricing strat → spoilage
>
>   Ⓖ % sales by item

Use some kind of visual designation as a signal when you have a graph, a table, or some other visual or set of data. That way, you'll know at a glance which tab to click back to when you need that data.

Try it again with the second tab:

Sales Breakout	**Vitamin Content**

E-mail from Sales Manager to Purchasing Supervisor:

Carrots, apples, and potatoes last a very long time in cold storage. I am a bit concerned about the lettuce, though; our farmers generally produce a higher volume of lettuce than of any other single item. The other items generally sell within acceptable time frames, even the tomatoes and bananas.

Customers do sometimes ask about the vitamin and nutrient content of various items. Maybe I should post the data on the pricing signs? Here's some data on the vitamin A and vitamin C content of our produce:

Vitamin Content of Produce Items Sold at Produce Stand P in April		
	Vitamin C content	**Vitamin A content**
Apples	low	low
Bananas	medium	low
Carrots	low	high
Lettuce	high	low
Oranges	high	medium
Potatoes	medium	low
Tomatoes	high	high

I also have research indicating that organic produce has a higher vitamin content than non-organic counterparts. I think that could be a very valuable marketing point.

In contrast to Table problems, MSR problems have static tables—you can't sort them. A map for the second tab might look like this:

> #2 Vit
>> Spoil: maybe lettuce
>> Ⓣ Vit A + C
>> Org = more Vit, +

So what? It sounds like lettuce might have spoilage or shelf-life issues, though the sales manager doesn't explicitly say so. Then there's a bunch of data on vitamin content; note that this data exists and that it's in the form high-medium-low (not numbers), but ignore the details until you get a question about it. Finally, the last couple of sentences introduce the idea that organic produce could be a positive selling point.

Take a moment to think about how the two tabs connect; feel free to click back and forth to glance at the info again. The supervisor asks some questions and the manager responds to those questions. The two visuals contain the same list of fruits and vegetables (though not in the same order—be careful). It isn't clear at this point how the sales data and the vitamin content data might otherwise connect, so wait to see what questions you're asked.

Here are the two tabs again, along with the first question:

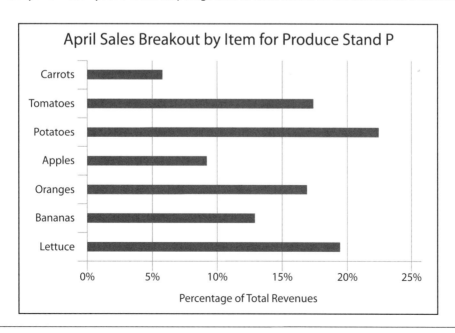

| **Sales Breakout** | **Vitamin Content** |

E-mail from Purchasing Supervisor to Sales Manager:

Total April sales for your produce stand were $4,441; the itemized data is below.

We already know that customers base their purchasing decisions on whether something is in season and how much it costs. Management believes that customers also care about the health factor, such as how high the vitamin content is for different types of produce. Do you have any data that could help us to evaluate this question?

We also need to think about pricing strategies in light of the fact that some items have a far longer shelf life. Potatoes will last weeks in cold storage, while the tomatoes won't last more than a few days without suffering a reduction in quality. Please send me any information you have about spoilage rates or other factors we should consider when setting prices.

April Sales Breakout by Item for Produce Stand P

(Percentage of Total Revenues)

Sales Breakout	**Vitamin Content**

E-mail from Sales Manager to Purchasing Supervisor:

Carrots, apples, and potatoes last a very long time in cold storage. I am a bit concerned about the lettuce, though; our farmers generally produce a higher volume of lettuce than of any other single item. The other items generally sell within acceptable time frames, even the tomatoes and bananas.

Customers do sometimes ask about the vitamin and nutrient content of various items. Maybe I should post the data on the pricing signs? Here's some data on the vitamin A and vitamin C content of our produce:

Vitamin Content of Produce Items Sold at Produce Stand P in April		
	Vitamin C content	*Vitamin A content*
Apples	low	low
Bananas	medium	low
Carrots	low	high
Lettuce	high	low
Oranges	high	medium
Potatoes	medium	low
Tomatoes	high	high

I also have research indicating that organic produce has a higher vitamin content than non-organic counterparts. I think that could be a very valuable marketing point.

For each of the following, select *Justified* if it is a justified inference on the basis of the information provided. Otherwise, select *Not justified*.

Justified	Not justified	
○	○	Some of Produce Stand P's lettuce may spoil or be in danger of spoiling before it is all sold.
○	○	More bananas than apples are sold at Produce Stand P.
○	○	Produce high in vitamin A, vitamin C, or both accounted for more than half of April revenues at Produce Stand P.

This is an either-or question, the exact same format you saw for Table questions. These questions always present answers in the form *either X or Y*, such as true/false, yes/no, or, as in this case, justified/not justified. Three statements will accompany the question; your task is to choose a single answer for each statement. In order to earn credit for this question, you have to answer all three statements correctly.

This question specifically asks whether the statement is a *justified inference*. These statements will not be found directly in the tabs; rather, you will have to determine whether something is reasonably justified, or able to be proven, based upon related information from the prompt.

Next, scan through the three statements. On some problems, the statements are very similar and can be solved simultaneously or very similarly. On others, the statements are independent and must be solved separately.

In this case, the statements each address different aspects of the information provided, so work through them individually. Here's the first statement:

Justified	Not justified	
○	○	Some of Produce Stand P's lettuce may spoil or be in danger of spoiling before it is all sold.

This statement talks about lettuce spoilage. Where do you need to go to find this information? Glance at your map. Spoilage was mentioned in both tabs.

Step 2: Plan Your Approach

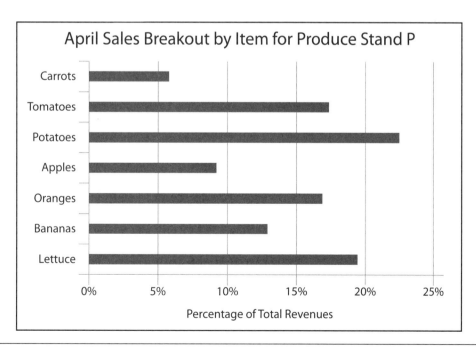

Sales Breakout   **Vitamin Content**

E-mail from Purchasing Supervisor to Sales Manager:

Total April sales for your produce stand were $4,441; the itemized data is below.

We already know that customers base their purchasing decisions on whether something is in season and how much it costs. Management believes that customers also care about the health factor, such as how high the vitamin content is for different types of produce. Do you have any data that could help us to evaluate this question?

We also need to think about pricing strategies in light of the fact that some items have a far longer shelf life. Potatoes will last weeks in cold storage, while the tomatoes won't last more than a few days without suffering a reduction in quality. Please send me any information you have about spoilage rates or other factors we should consider when setting prices.

April Sales Breakout by Item for Produce Stand P

Carrots
Tomatoes
Potatoes
Apples
Oranges
Bananas
Lettuce

0%   5%   10%   15%   20%   25%
Percentage of Total Revenues

Sales Breakout	Vitamin Content

E-mail from Sales Manager to Purchasing Supervisor:

Carrots, apples, and potatoes last a very long time in cold storage. I am a bit concerned about the lettuce, though; our farmers generally produce a higher volume of lettuce than of any other single item. The other items generally sell within acceptable time frames, even the tomatoes and bananas.

Customers do sometimes ask about the vitamin and nutrient content of various items. Maybe I should post the data on the pricing signs? Here's some data on the vitamin A and vitamin C content of our produce:

Vitamin Content of Produce Items Sold at Produce Stand P in April		
	Vitamin C content	*Vitamin A content*
Apples	low	low
Bananas	medium	low
Carrots	low	high
Lettuce	high	low
Oranges	high	medium
Potatoes	medium	low
Tomatoes	high	high

I also have research indicating that organic produce has a higher vitamin content than non-organic counterparts. I think that could be a very valuable marketing point.

6

The *Sales Breakout* tab mentioned spoilage and the *Vitamin Content* tab specifically mentioned lettuce, so you'll need both to answer the question. Find and reread the relevant text:

> (Sales Breakout Tab): We also need to think about pricing strategies in light of the fact that some items have a far longer shelf life. Potatoes will last weeks in cold storage, while the tomatoes won't last more than a few days without suffering a reduction in quality. Please send me any information you have about spoilage rates or other factors we should consider when setting prices.

> (Vitamin Content Tab) Carrots, apples, and potatoes last a very long time in cold storage. I am a bit concerned about the lettuce, though; our farmers generally produce a higher volume of lettuce than of any other single item. The other items generally sell within acceptable time frames, even the tomatoes and bananas.

Step 3: Solve the Problem

The supervisor points out that some items will last much longer than others, then asks about spoilage rates, implying that some items may spoil or be in danger of spoiling. The sales manager indicates that certain items do last a long time, but he is *concerned about the lettuce*. He also indicates that the *other items generally sell within acceptable time frames*, implying that the lettuce might *not* sell within an acceptable time frame; that is, it might spoil before it can be sold. The first statement, then, is *Justified*.

Evaluate the second and third statements in the same manner, repeating your UPS steps each time:

Justified	Not justified	
◯	◯	More bananas than apples are sold at Produce Stand P.

Careful! The bar graph in the *Sales Breakout* tab shows information about sales *revenues*, not sales *volume*. While it is true that banana sales revenues were higher than apple sales revenues, the prompt does not indicate the relative number of items sold. It could be that more apples than bananas were sold, but the price per banana was higher, such that total banana revenue was higher. The second statement is *Not justified*. Now, here's the third statement:

Justified	Not justified	
◯	◯	Produce high in vitamin A, vitamin C, or both accounted for more than half of April revenues at Produce Stand P.

Note first that the question asks whether this group accounted for *more than half* of revenues. You will not necessarily have to calculate the exact figure; it will be enough if you can tell whether it is more or less than half. The *Vitamin Content* tab has the vitamin data; the *Sales Breakout* tab has the sales data. You're going to have to combine the two tabs.

First, go to *Vitamin Content* and look for the items that are high in either or both of the vitamins: carrots, lettuce, oranges, and tomatoes. The remaining items—apples, bananas, and potatoes—are not high in either vitamin. Jot the items in two clearly labeled lists: high-V and not-high-V. Since you are comparing to 50%, you could sum for either group.

Next, click on *Sales Breakout* and find the percentage of revenue for each item. It is easier to sum three categories than four, so eyeball the bars for the not-high-vitamin items: Do they sum to less than 50%?

$$A < 10\%$$
$$B < 15\%$$
$$\underline{P < 25\%}$$
$$\text{sum} < 50\%$$

The not-high-vitamin items account for less than half of revenues, so the high-vitamin items account for more than half of revenues.

Alternatively, eyeball the bars for the high-vitamin items. If you approximate or round down and the sum is still greater than 50%, the statement must be true.

$$C > 5\%$$
$$L > 15\%$$
$$O > 15\%$$
$$\underline{T > 15\%}$$
$$\text{sum} > 50\%$$

Even if you round each bar down to the closest grid line, the sum is still 50%. The longest bar is actually closer to 20%, so this sum will definitely cross the 50% threshold. Therefore, the third statement is *Justified*.

The answers are as follows:

Justified	Not justified	
◉	○	Some of Produce Stand P's lettuce may spoil or be in danger of spoiling before it is all sold.
○	◉	More bananas than apples are sold at Produce Stand P.
◉	○	Produce high in vitamin A, vitamin C, or both accounted for more than half of April revenues at Produce Stand P.

Here is a second question for the same prompt; try out the UPS process yourself.

In the month of April, Produce Stand P generated approximately how much revenue, in dollars, from items that were high in both vitamin A and vitamin C?

(A) $775

(B) $1,280

(C) $1,575

(D) $2,080

(E) $2,875

Sales Breakout | **Vitamin Content**

E-mail from Purchasing Supervisor to Sales Manager:

Total April sales for your produce stand were $4,441; the itemized data is below.

We already know that customers base their purchasing decisions on whether something is in season and how much it costs. Management believes that customers also care about the health factor, such as how high the vitamin content is for different types of produce. Do you have any data that could help us to evaluate this question?

We also need to think about pricing strategies in light of the fact that some items have a far longer shelf life. Potatoes will last weeks in cold storage, while the tomatoes won't last more than a few days without suffering a reduction in quality. Please send me any information you have about spoilage rates or other factors we should consider when setting prices.

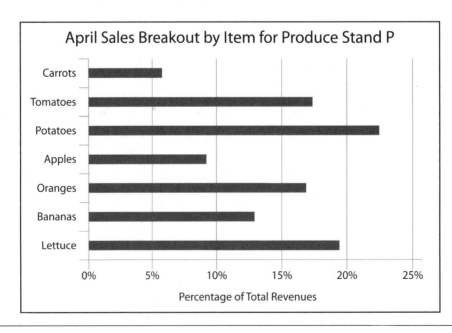

April Sales Breakout by Item for Produce Stand P

Sales Breakout	Vitamin Content

E-mail from Sales Manager to Purchasing Supervisor:

Carrots, apples, and potatoes last a very long time in cold storage. I am a bit concerned about the lettuce, though; our farmers generally produce a higher volume of lettuce than of any other single item. The other items generally sell within acceptable time frames, even the tomatoes and bananas.

Customers do sometimes ask about the vitamin and nutrient content of various items. Maybe I should post the data on the pricing signs? Here's some data on the vitamin A and vitamin C content of our produce:

Vitamin Content of Produce Items Sold at Produce Stand P in April		
	Vitamin C content	*Vitamin A content*
Apples	low	low
Bananas	medium	low
Carrots	low	high
Lettuce	high	low
Oranges	high	medium
Potatoes	medium	low
Tomatoes	high	high

I also have research indicating that organic produce has a higher vitamin content than non-organic counterparts. I think that could be a very valuable marketing point.

First, make sure you understand the question. You'll need to find items that are high in *both* vitamins A and C (*not* items high in just one or the other).

Second, plan how to answer the question. You'll need to use *Vitamin Content* to find those items high in both vitamin A and C. To calculate the revenue, add up the percentages of sales for the relevant items and then multiply by the dollar figure given for total sales in the first paragraph of the *Sales Breakout* tab. Lay these steps out on your scrap paper.

Finally, go ahead and solve. Only tomatoes are high in *both* vitamins A and C. Tomatoes accounted for approximately 17%–18% of total revenues (glance at those answers; you don't need to be very precise), so pull up the calculator and plug in this calculation: $0.17 \times 4{,}441 = 754.97$.

The closest match in the answers is $775. The correct answer is (A).

If you feel comfortable working by hand, the answers are far enough apart to estimate pretty roughly. For example, 10% of $4,441 is about $444, so 20% is about $888. The answer has to be close to but less than $888; only answer (A) matches.

Review and Improve on MSR

The Understand–Plan–Solve process will help you both to answer the question and to review your work afterwards. If you answer a question incorrectly—or aren't fully confident about something you answered correctly—review each step of the process.

First, did you properly understand everything? Did you overlook, misunderstand, or fail to comprehend any information in the prompt? How was your map; should you have included something that you didn't write down, or did you get too far into the detail? Did you miss any connections between different tabs or pieces of information? Did you answer the question that was asked?

What about your plan? Was there an easier or more efficient way to approach the problem? And did you make any mistakes at the solution stage?

Try another MSR problem set to test your skills. This time, you'll do all three questions first. A word of warning: The prompt is extremely technical. Often, when this happens, the questions themselves *don't* require you to dive very deeply into the technical details. Use that knowledge to your advantage as you work through this problem set.

Ready? Set a timer for 9 minutes and go!

| **Proposal** | **Purpose** | **Budget** |

The government of Storinia has proposed to conduct three particle physics experiments in Antarctica, as described below.

The *ultra-high-energy cosmic ray detector* (UHECR-D) will track a variety of subatomic particles with exceptionally high kinetic energy traveling from outer space by recording secondary showers of particles created by these UHECRs as they collide with the upper atmosphere of Earth.

The *polyethylene naphthalate neutrino observatory* (PEN-NO) will search for neutrinos, extremely light and fast subatomic particles that interact only weakly with normal matter. To prevent false-positive results from cosmic rays, PEN-NO will be buried deep below the ice.

The *magnetic monopole detector* (MaMoD) will attempt to verify the existence of magnetic monopoles, hypothetical subatomic particles that some physical theories postulate are left over from the creation of the universe.

| Proposal | **Purpose** | Budget |

The purpose of UHECR-D is to ascertain the identity, composition, and extraterrestrial origin of ultra-high-energy cosmic rays, which are much less prevalent and well-understood than lower-energy cosmic rays. PEN-NO will measure the mass and speed of neutrinos produced in particle accelerators and nuclear reactors, both to reduce uncertainty in the known mass of a neutrino and to contribute to the resolution of a recent challenge to Einstein's theory of relativity posed by the observation of neutrinos supposedly traveling slightly faster than light. PEN-NO will also measure the passage of solar and other neutrinos of astronomical origin. Finally, if MaMoD is successful in its search, it will provide experimental proof for Dirac's explanation of charge quantization and fix an asymmetry in Maxwell's equations of electromagnetism.

Purpose	Proposal	Budget

The government of Storinia projects that it will cost $42 million in total and take 2 years to construct UHECR-D, PEN-NO, and MaMoD. The government also projects that once construction is finished, the annual operating budget for each experiment will be $3.6 million for UHECR-D, $4.3 million for PEN-NO, and $2.7 million for MaMoD. All these figures are in real 2015 dollars (removing the effect of predicted inflation).

1. For each of the following statements, select *Yes* if the statement is supported by the evidence provided. Otherwise, select *No*.

Yes	No	
○	○	With a construction budget of $30 million, the Storinian government will be able to search for proof of an explanation of charge quantization and help resolve a controversy by measuring the speed of neutrinos produced in nuclear reactors.
○	○	In its Antarctic experiments, the Storinian government will attempt to ascertain the mass and speed of cosmic rays.
○	○	If the PEN-NO experiment operates on the surface of the ice in Antarctica, its findings will be considered more valid than those produced by the experiment as currently envisioned.

2. According to the information provided, the proposed measurement of which of the following kinds of particles is intended to improve the estimate of the mass of these particles?

   (A) Ultra-high-energy cosmic rays

   (B) Particles created by UHECRs above the Earth

   (C) Neutrinos produced in nuclear reactors

   (D) Neutrinos that originate in the Sun

   (E) Magnetic monopoles

3. For each of the following particle types, select *Can conclude* if you can conclude from the information provided that the particles in question have a negligible effect on ordinary matter. Otherwise, select *Cannot conclude*.

Can conclude	Cannot conclude	
○	○	Ultra-high-energy cosmic rays
○	○	Neutrinos produced in particle accelerators
○	○	Magnetic monopoles

How did it go? Before reading the following explanations, review your work yourself.

Before you check the correct answers, evaluate how you think you did. Where are you confident and where are you unsure? What felt cumbersome to analyze or process, and can you think of any way to make that cumbersome part easier? Do you want to try any of the problems (or parts of problems) again? Go ahead. This time, you don't even need to time yourself. Take as much time as you want.

Next, check the correct answers but nothing else. (You'll have to scroll down a bit—we didn't want to give away the answers too soon.) Does knowing the answers give you any ideas about what else to try—or what might have gone wrong—on any part of any problem? If so, dig in to see whether you can figure things out on your own. Whenever you can do this, you'll remember the lesson a lot more easily.

Finally, use the explanations. Start to read through, but stop as soon as you read something that gives you an idea. Try to push that idea as far as you can before you go back to the explanation for more. Again, the more you figure out for yourself, the easier it will be for you to remember what you're learning.

Ready for the official explanations? Let's go!

Step 1: Understand the Prompt and Question

As you review the solution, check whether your reasoning and understanding were accurate, not just whether you answered the question correctly. Sometimes, you get lucky—it is a multiple-choice test, after all.

The long-hand text below summarizes what someone might think while reading each tab. A sample map is shown at the end.

Proposal tab:

> *Storinia is planning 3 experiments in Antarctica.*
>
> *I don't understand a lot of these words. That's okay—ignore them.*
>
> *(Glancing down.) One paragraph per experiment. Right now, I just need a basic understanding. Hopefully I won't ever need to really understand this detail.*
>
> *#1 is something about outer space coming to Earth.*
>
> *#2 will be buried in ice.*
>
> *#3 is something about magnetic something that has to do with the creation of the universe.*

Purpose tab:

> *The name of the tab is* Purpose, *so presumably they're going to tell me the purpose of at least some of these experiments.*
>
> *(Glancing down.) All three acronyms are listed in this paragraph.*
>
> *The details here are really hard. Big picture only.*
>
> *#1 is something about a certain type of cosmic ray that isn't well understood—what is it, what's it made of, where it comes from.*
>
> *#2 involves learning more about neutrinos and something about Einstein's theory of relativity.*
>
> *#3 is searching for something; if successful, it will prove one theory and fix another.*

Budget tab:

> *What the experiments will cost and how long they'll take to start.*
>
> *Also provides annual operating costs for each one.*

Here is one version of a map for this prompt. The first line of the first tab indicates that it will discuss three experiments, so consider using a table to organize the information by experiment and by tab.

Exp	T1 Prop	T2 Purp	T3 Budg
UHECR-D	space to Earth	made of? come from? high-energy cosmic ray	$3.6m annual
PEN-NO	neutrinos below ice	mass and speed Einstein th. relativity	$4.3m ann
MaMoD	exist? creation of universe	prove D's theory (CQ) fix M's eqns	$2.7m ann
All			$42m initial 2 yrs

You will likely gain additional understanding as you continue through the material. For instance, part of *UHECR-D* does stand for *high-energy cosmic ray*, but the significance of these words doesn't really become apparent until the *Purpose* tab—so you might not write them down until you get to that point. You could also go back and add them under the *Proposal* tab entry.

First, here are all of the correct answers:

Question 1: No, No, No

Question 2: (C)

Question 3: Cannot, Can, Cannot

Any ideas? Go test them out before you continue on with the explanations.

1.   For each of the following statements, select *Yes* if the statement is supported by the evidence provided. Otherwise, select *No*.

The question asks whether, using information from the tabs, you can support, or prove true, the given statements.

Glance through them to see whether the statements are related in any way. They are not, so solve each one individually.

This kind of question is basically a "search and match" exercise. Read the statement first, then use your map to figure out where to look in the tabs to try to prove the statement. Here is the first statement:

Yes	No	
○	○	With a construction budget of $30 million, the Storinian government will be able to search for proof of an explanation of charge quantization and help resolve a controversy by measuring the speed of neutrinos produced in nuclear reactors.

The overall construction budget was $42m, so $30m is a subset of this budget. The question is asking whether this subset will be sufficient to accomplish just a certain part of the job. Which part?

Step 2: Plan Your Approach

Wait! Before you get into the annoying technical details, review the monetary information you were given. Tab 3 provides the *annual* budget to operate each separate experiment, but the initial *construction* budget was never split up by experiment—it's $42m for all three together. No information is given to allow you to assume, for example, that each will cost roughly the same to construct or, alternatively, that the ratio of construction costs will mirror the ratio of operating costs. The facilities for any one experiment could cost more or less than $30m to construct.

Step 3: Solve the Problem

That's it! The answer to the first statement is *No*: This is not supported by the given evidence.

If you messed anything up, pinpoint the specific mistake(s) and figure out what you could do differently to avoid that mistake in the future.

Alternatively, maybe you answered this correctly but realize in hindsight that you spent more time than necessary to do so. How could you save time next time? For instance, if you spent time digging into the detail on the experiments before realizing that you didn't need any of that to address the statement, then remind yourself next time to slow down and apply the process. Understand and plan before you try to solve.

Repeat your review of all three steps as you work through the second statement:

Yes	No	
○	○	In its Antarctic experiments, the Storinian government will attempt to ascertain the mass and speed of cosmic rays.

Hmm. All three experiments take place in the Antarctic. This question is asking whether one certain thing is planned for one of these experiments. Which one?

This time you do have to get a bit into the details. You've got two different sets of key words you could go with: either *mass and speed* or *cosmic rays*. Glance at your map.

And here's where your first big clue comes in! *Cosmic rays* are the first experiment, but *mass and speed* go with the second experiment. It looks like this choice might be a **Mix-Up** trap: It mixes up text from two different parts of the prompt, creating a statement that the passage didn't actually say.

Here's the sentence on cosmic rays:

> *The purpose of UHECR-D is to ascertain the identity, composition, and extraterrestrial origin of ultra-high-energy cosmic rays, which are much less prevalent and well-understood than lower-energy cosmic rays.*

This sentence says nothing about either *mass* or *speed*.

It's enough to check just the part that discusses cosmic rays, since the statement does specify this type of particle. But you can also check the part that describes the second experiment:

> *PEN-NO will measure the mass and speed of neutrinos produced in particle accelerators and nuclear reactors, both to reduce uncertainty in the known mass of a neutrino and to contribute to the resolution of a recent challenge to Einstein's theory of relativity posed by the observation of neutrinos supposedly traveling slightly faster than light. PEN-NO will also measure the passage of solar and other neutrinos of astronomical origin.*

Mass and speed are mentioned, but not *cosmic rays*. This part is all about something called a neutrino.

Indeed, this is a mix-up trap! They jammed together information about two different types of particles, hoping that people would remember reading about both *cosmic rays* and *mass and speed* and just assume that this meant the statement could be supported. If you fell for this trap, this is a good reminder to make sure that you check the proof in the source material—every time! Don't just rely on your memory; the test writers know people do this and they set traps accordingly.

The correct answer for the second statement is *No*: The statement is not supported by the given information.

Here's the third statement:

Yes	No	
○	○	If the PEN-NO experiment operates on the surface of the ice in Antarctica, its findings will be considered more valid than those produced by the experiment as currently envisioned.

This problem explicitly mentions the second experiment—great. The statement asks whether changing a certain condition (operating *on the surface of the ice*) would lead to a better outcome. Glance at your map. The first tab mentioned something about being *below the ice*. Go back and scan for that text.

> *To prevent false-positive results from cosmic rays, PEN-NO will be buried deep below the ice.*

It was a conscious choice, then, to conduct the experiment below the ice: Doing so will prevent a certain bad outcome. If that is the case, then moving the experiment to the surface of the ice might allow that bad outcome to occur, so the results would *not* be better.

The correct answer for the third statement is *No*: This is not supported by the information given in the prompt.

The third statement was similar to an Inference question. The passage doesn't say outright that conducting the experiment on the surface wouldn't be as beneficial. Rather, you have to infer from the stated information to arrive at that conclusion.

Here are the correct answers for the first question:

1. For each of the following statements, select *Yes* if the statement is supported by the evidence provided. Otherwise, select *No*.

Yes	No	
○	◉	With a construction budget of $30 million, the Storinian government will be able to search for proof of an explanation of charge quantization and help resolve a controversy by measuring the speed of neutrinos produced in nuclear reactors.
○	◉	In its Antarctic experiments, the Storinian government will attempt to ascertain the mass and speed of cosmic rays.
○	◉	If the PEN-NO experiment operates on the surface of the ice in Antarctica, its findings will be considered more valid than those produced by the experiment as currently envisioned.

6

UPS Redux

Repeat the process with the second question. This one is a standard multiple-choice problem:

2. According to the information provided, the proposed measurement of which of the following kinds of particles is intended to improve the estimate of the mass of these particles?

    (A) Ultra-high-energy cosmic rays

    (B) Particles created by UHECRs above the Earth

    (C) Neutrinos produced in nuclear reactors

    (D) Neutrinos that originate in the Sun

    (E) Magnetic monopoles

This problem asks for a certain kind of particle that fits the question information. Glance at the answers—the first two are cosmic rays, the next two are neutrinos, and the last is magnetic monopoles. So the first thing to figure out is this: Which experiment is the question referring to?

The particles are going to be measured and that measurement is going to *improve the estimate of the mass*. That is, measure the particles and get a better idea of the mass of those particles.

Glance at your map. The second experiment, PEN-NO, talked about the mass of particles, so start there. The particles for this experiment are neutrinos, so it looks like the answer will probably be (C) or (D), but dive into the text to confirm this.

> *PEN-NO will measure the mass and speed of neutrinos produced in particle accelerators and nuclear reactors, both to reduce uncertainty in the known mass of a neutrino and to . . . PEN-NO will also measure the passage of solar and other neutrinos of astronomical origin.*

First, it is the neutrinos: *Reduce uncertainty in the known mass* is a synonym for *improve the estimate of the mass*. Eliminate answers (A), (B), and (E) for talking about the wrong type of particle. The next sentence does mention solar neutrinos but says only that the experiment will measure the *passage* of these neutrinos, not their mass.

The correct answer is (C): neutrinos produced in nuclear reactors.

While the answer choices for this question appear to imply that you have to get into all of the technical detail, you really don't have to go very far. The key word *mass* allows you to narrow down to two answers pretty quickly. And choosing between just two answers is not nearly as hard as evaluating all five.

You're back to either-or for the third problem:

3. For each of the following particle types, select *Can conclude* if you can conclude from the information provided that the particles in question have a negligible effect on ordinary matter. Otherwise, select *Cannot conclude*.

Each of the statements accompanying the question stem is one of the three types of particles discussed in the prompt. This question asks whether the information given in the prompt allows you to conclude that each type of particle has *a negligible effect on ordinary matter*.

What does *a negligible effect on ordinary matter* even mean? In general, if you don't really understand what's going on, don't move to plan or solve. Just guess and move on.

If you do want to tackle this problem, a *negligible* effect means an unimportant or minor effect. Next, where could that information be? The third tab was all about budget, so it won't be there. The first tab describes the particles themselves and the second describes the experiments. The desired information could be in either tab, so start with the first tab.

The first description is about cosmic rays but says nothing about ordinary matter. Flip over to the second tab. The first sentence provides more information about cosmic rays but still says nothing about ordinary matter, so you *cannot conclude* anything about the effect cosmic rays have on ordinary matter.

Go back to the first tab to see what it says about *neutrinos produced in particle accelerators*. This tab says that neutrinos in general *interact only weakly with normal matter*. That almost matches what the question stem says—it's not a very important effect. In this case, you *can conclude* that *neutrinos produced in particle accelerators* have a *negligible effect on ordinary matter*.

Finally, check what the text says about magnetic monopoles. The first tab doesn't mention ordinary matter in connection with these particles, nor does the second tab. As a result, you *cannot conclude* anything about the effect magnetic monopoles have on ordinary matter. Here are the correct answers for the third question:

3. For each of the following particle types, select *Can conclude* if you can conclude from the information provided that the particles in question have a negligible effect on ordinary matter. Otherwise, select *Cannot conclude*.

Can conclude	Cannot conclude	
○	◉	Ultra-high-energy cosmic rays
◉	○	Neutrinos produced in particle accelerators
○	◉	Magnetic monopoles

That was a very challenging MSR prompt. If you struggled with it, notice a couple of things that might help you next time around.

First, while the tabs did have extremely detailed scientific information, you didn't have to become an expert in particle physics in order to answer all of the questions. The technical language was often just window dressing. For instance, in problem 1, the first statement mentions all kinds of details (*charge quantization*??), but all you needed to know was that the prompt didn't provide any information regarding how much each of the three experiments would cost separately to build. Likewise, you can get through the second and third statements of the first question without having to understand all of the details.

The third question was pretty challenging—even the question stem itself was hard to parse. When you realize that you don't understand what the question is saying or asking, that's an excellent clue to get out. Guess randomly and move on!

If you feel okay with this subject matter, then even the third question requires only a medium understanding of the text. The one statement that did match used close synonyms (e.g., *ordinary matter* in the question and *normal matter* in the prompt). The descriptions for the other two particles don't mention any kind of interactions with any matter at all. The test writers want to see whether you can read around the scary technical language and still process the high-level information.

This fits a lot of what happens in the real world, too. You run up against some really technical detail at work, and you may have to understand it well enough to make a high-level business call about something— but you don't suddenly have to become an expert about this technical thing. Expect that to happen on MSR as well.

Finally, when you're done answering any question, your learning has just begun. Take the time to pick apart the prompt, the question, and your own reasoning in order to get better the next time you tackle an intricate science MSR question.

And remember: Getting better also involves knowing what *not* to do so that you can guess and move on quickly. Use that precious time to better advantage elsewhere in the section!

Practice Your Skills

Log into Atlas for additional practice problems. Give yourself a block of time to do an entire MSR prompt plus three problems—review after you're done with the whole set for that prompt, not after each problem.

CHAPTER 7

Two-Part Analysis

In This Chapter

- UPS for Quant Two-Parts

- UPS for Verbal Two-Parts

- UPS for Logic Two-Parts

In this chapter, you will learn how to Understand–Plan–Solve your way to the answer for all three types of Two-Part problems: quant-, verbal-, and logic-based.

CHAPTER 7 Two-Part Analysis

Two-Part Analysis problems closely resemble regular multiple-choice questions on the Quant and Verbal sections of the exam—with a twist. As the name implies, the question you will answer will have two parts to it, not just one.

The prompt will appear at the top of the screen, followed by the question. The multiple-choice answers will appear in a table below that, as shown here:

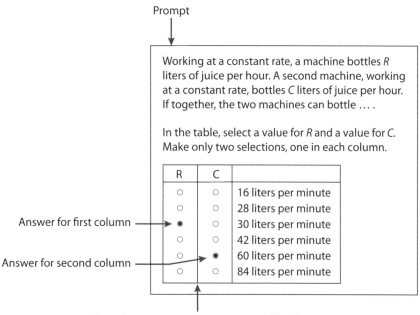

Prompt

Working at a constant rate, a machine bottles *R* liters of juice per hour. A second machine, working at a constant rate, bottles *C* liters of juice per hour. If together, the two machines can bottle … .

In the table, select a value for *R* and a value for *C*. Make only two selections, one in each column.

R	C	
○	○	16 liters per minute
○	○	28 liters per minute
●	○	30 liters per minute
○	○	42 liters per minute
○	●	60 liters per minute
○	○	84 liters per minute

Answer for first column

Answer for second column

Question: two-part, 5 or 6 answers offered; must answer both parts correctly to earn credit

The prompt will often feel very similar to a standard quant or verbal problem, but will likely contain more information than the typical quant or verbal problem. In addition, the two questions will likely be related or adjacent in some way, since you have to choose from the same set of answers for each question. For example, you might be asked to strengthen *and* weaken an argument, and all of the answers would be statements. However, the questions could be quite different, as long as the set of answers logically follows both questions. For example, a set of numerical answers in units of *boxes per hour* might accompany two dissimilar rate questions, such as the rate at which machine X operated *and* the rate at which the night crew fell short of a production goal.

You'll be given five or six answer choices and the correct answer for each part could actually be the same answer (though this is rare). At times, you may be asked to solve for the answers simultaneously; for example, you may need to solve for the interest rate for Investment A and the interest rate for Investment B, which together earned a given amount of interest.

Two-Parts typically fall fairly cleanly into one of three categories: quant-, verbal-, or logic-based. Some problems incorporate elements from two categories, but it's usually the case that you can identify the problem as primarily quant-based or primarily verbal-based and work accordingly.

UPS for Quant Two-Parts

Here's how to apply the Understand–Plan–Solve process to a quant-based Two-Part.

Try this problem:

> Two water storage tanks, Tank Alpha and Tank Bravo, can each hold more than 20,000 liters of water. Currently, Alpha contains 5,000 liters of water and Bravo contains 8,000 liters. Alpha will be filled at a constant rate of *A* liters per hour and Bravo will be filled at a constant rate of *B* liters per hour. If both tanks begin to be filled at the same time, after 15 hours, the two tanks will contain the same amount of water, though neither will be full.
>
> In the table below, identify a value for *A* and a value for *B* that together are consistent with the given information. Make only one selection in each column.

A	B	
○	○	30
○	○	90
○	○	150
○	○	220
○	○	290

Ready? Let's go!

Step 1: Understand the Prompt and Question

Before you start to read a Two-Part prompt, glance at the answers. What form are they in? In this case, they're numbers. Glance also at the question stem; it asks for the value of *A* and the value of *B*. This quick glance will give you an early clue that you've got a quant-based problem.

Treat this as you would a standard math story problem and translate the information carefully on your scratch paper. A quick sketch can help keep the information straight:

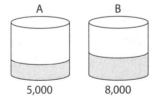

The two tanks are filling at different rates. In 15 hours, they'll have the same amount of water. What does that tell you about the rate for each tank?

Because Alpha has less water than Bravo to start, it must be filling at a faster rate—otherwise, Tank A couldn't catch up to Tank B. Jot a note on your scrap paper that *A* > *B*. If your answers don't match that idea, then you'll know you made a mistake somewhere.

The question stem contains an important clue: It specifically tells you to find values that *together are consistent* with the details given in the problem. As you move forward, look for opportunities to solve for the two values in tandem.

Step 2: Plan Your Approach

This is a work problem, so consider the RTW formula: Rate × Time = Work.

How are you going to go from a starting point of 5,000 and 8,000 liters to an ending point of the same number of liters?

Alpha has 5,000 liters now and will be filled at a rate of A liters per hour for 15 hours…hmm. If you ignore Bravo, that's not enough to solve for A. It is the case that you're going to need to solve for the two variables simultaneously.

There are two possible approaches. First, you could do algebra. Use the given variables to set up a mathematical representation for the final number of liters for Tank Alpha, at a rate of A, and the final number of liters for Tank Bravo, at a rate of B. Then, set those two numbers equal.

Second, you could try the answer choices. You know rate A must be greater than rate B, so try setting $B = 30$, the smallest value in the answers, and work from there.

On this particular problem, it's possible for the value of B to be one of four answer choices (everything but 290). In addition, since the two rates are connected, you cannot solve just to find B. In other words, you might actually have to try all four possibilities before you find the answer. In this case, an algebraic approach is likely to be more efficient.

Step 3: Solve the Problem

Tank Alpha is filling at the rate of A liters per hour. Over 15 hours, it will add $15A$ liters. It started with 5,000 liters, so Alpha's final amount of water is equal to $5,000 + 15A$.

If Tank Bravo is filling at the rate of B liters per hour, then it will wind up with $8,000 + 15B$ liters. Now, set the equations equal to each other:

$$5,000 + 15A = 8,000 + 15B$$

That equation can't be solved for A and B individually—this is why you have to solve simultaneously. There are multiple possible solutions, but there is a consistent relationship between the two rates. Your task is to figure out what that relationship is. Only one *pair* of answer choices will fit that relationship.

$$5,000 + 15A = 8,000 + 15B$$
$$15A = 3,000 + 15B \quad \text{Subtract 5,000 from each side.}$$
$$15A - 15B = 3,000 \quad \text{Subtract } 15B \text{ from each side.}$$
$$A - B = 200 \quad \text{Divide both sides by 15.}$$

7

This is the relationship between the two rates: They have to differ by 200, and *A* must be greater than *B*. Look at the answers. The only pairing that works is 90 and 290:

A	B	
○	○	30
○	●	90
○	○	150
○	○	220
●	○	290

Double-check that you filled in the right columns with the appropriate numbers! Alpha has to fill faster, so *A* has to be the greater rate.

UPS for Verbal Two-Parts

Verbal Two-Parts most often feel similar to Critical Reasoning (CR) problems from the Verbal section.

As always, the UPS process will help you to both answer the question and review your work afterwards. Whether you answer the question correctly or incorrectly, use UPS to review each step of the process afterwards.

Try this problem:

> Software Company M accused Company S of intellectual property theft, citing as evidence similar user interface designs for the company's new operating system products, both of which launched this year, and the fact that Company M's chief designer defected to Company S nine months ago. Company S countered that the product was 90% completed by the time the former chief designer joined Company S and that the designer was not allowed to work on that product in order to avoid any potential conflicts of interest.
>
> Select the additional information that, if true, would provide the strongest evidence *For* Company S's claim that it did not illegally obtain information about Company M's products, and select the additional information that, if true, would provide the strongest evidence *Against* that claim.

For	Against	
○	○	A comparison with a third operating system company's user interface design shows overlap with Company M only in features that have been in industry-wide use for years.
○	○	Company S's former chief designer quit after a dispute over creative control.
○	○	Last year, another company released software that incorporates some of the same user interface designs at issue in the dispute.
○	○	Several key parts of the software code in Company S's product are nearly identical to code that Company M's former chief designer wrote for Company M.
○	○	It is quite common for software companies to accuse other companies of intellectual property theft.

How did it go? Before reading the explanations below, review your work yourself. Then, use the walk-through below to help you past any sticking points or to help you brainstorm more efficient approaches to your solution process.

Step 1: Understand the Prompt and Question

Glance at the answers: The fact that there are sentences indicate that this is likely either a verbal- or logic-based problem. The next clue: The question asks for evidence *For* something and evidence *Against* something. This is similar to a Critical Reasoning problem from the Verbal section, so tackle this in the same way that you tackle CR.

Read the argument and make a map:

> M: S stole our design
>
> 1. Similar design
>
> 2. M's designer → S
>
> S: 90% done; designer not allowed to work on it

The first part of the question asks you to strengthen Company S's claim that it did *not* steal anything from Company M; in other words, the question is oriented from S's point of view, not M's. The second part asks you to weaken Company S's claim.

Step 2: Plan Your Approach

You can use the same strategies you use for CR problems. A correct Strengthen answer makes the conclusion at least a little more likely to be valid, so the first column will validate (at least a little) the claim that Company S did *not* steal from Company M. Look through the answers now, concentrating just on this part of the question.

Step 3: Solve the Problem

If you're very good at CR, you can try to find the strengthen and weaken answers at the same time. If, on the other hand, you have ever accidentally picked a strengthen answer when you were supposed to weaken, or vice versa, then concentrate on finding the *For* answer first. Then, go through again for the *Against* answer.

The answer choices are labeled (A) through (E) for clarity. As you read each one, ask yourself whether it makes Company S's case any better:

> (A) *A comparison with a third operating system company's user interface design shows overlap with Company M only in features that have been in industry-wide use for years.*

A third company's system doesn't overlap much with Company M's system. A *lack* of overlap doesn't strengthen Company S's case. If a third company's system were super similar to M's system, that might help S's case—but that's not what this choice says. Eliminate this answer.

> (B) *Company S's former chief designer quit after a dispute over creative control.*

Careful! The argument is about Company M's designer, the one who moved over to Company S. The reason Company S's former designer (a different person) quit has no bearing on what happened when Company M's designer joined. Eliminate this choice.

> (C) *Last year, another company released software that incorporates some of the same user interface designs at issue in the dispute.*

A third company released software *last* year that contains some of the designs that are in dispute. The argument states that Company M released its own software *this* year, so this certainly bolsters Company S's claim that it did not steal anything from Company M (though maybe they both stole ideas from the third company!). This one looks good but check the final two answers.

(D) *Several key parts of the software code in Company S's product are nearly identical to code that Company M's former chief designer wrote for Company M.*

If some parts of the software code are identical to code written by Company M's former chief designer while working for that company, this definitely does not help Company S's claim that it didn't steal any ideas. This might even *weaken* S's claim. Note that down. Also, eliminate this choice.

(E) *It is quite common for software companies to accuse other companies of intellectual property theft.*

This may be true in general, but it does not provide any evidence as to what happened in the specific case discussed in the argument.

The correct answer for the first part, *For*, is answer (C).

Now, reuse your initial analysis to help narrow down the answers faster for the second part. Which choice goes *against* S's claim that it didn't steal any ideas?

Start with answer (D), the one that you already thought might be a weaken. If parts of the code written by the employee who switched companies are *nearly identical* in the two products, this definitely weakens S's claim that it did not steal anything from M. It would be pretty unlikely for someone else to have written code that is *nearly identical* in *several key parts*.

Do review the other answers, just to be sure. For answer (A), this third company's design overlaps with M only on commonly used features. What impact does that have on the claim that S stole some of M's features? It's not clear what features M is claiming S stole, so this information about a third company is not relevant to the argument.

Answers (B) and (E) are irrelevant one way or the other, so they can't be the *Against* answer. If answer (C) is the *For* answer, then it can't also be the *Against* answer; these two classifications are opposites. So answer (D) must be correct.

The answers are:

For	Against	
O	O	A comparison with a third operating system company's user interface design shows overlap with Company M only in features that have been in industry-wide use for years.
O	O	Company S's former chief designer quit after a dispute over creative control.
●	O	Last year, another company released software that incorporates some of the same user interface designs at issue in the dispute.
O	●	Several key parts of the software code in Company S's product are nearly identical to code that Company M's former chief designer wrote for that company.
O	O	It is quite common for software companies to accuse other companies of intellectual property theft.

When the two parts of the question are not connected, as in the first verbal example above, you could save time by thinking about the two parts simultaneously—but you are taking a risk. If you ever make mistakes with this (e.g., if you swapped the two answers on the last problem), then tackle the two questions separately in the future.

Some Two-Part questions will ask for two connected answers, as you saw in the quant-based question earlier, and this can happen on a verbal-based problem, too. For example, you might be asked to find a specific *Cause* and *Effect* sequence or a certain *Circumstance* that would lead to a specific *Prediction*. In these cases, you must think about the two parts of the question simultaneously.

Try another one:

> The Golden Age of Radio—the period of time during which radio broadcasting in the United States reached its widest audience—came to an end in the 1950s as radio was supplanted by television. World War II, which had caused widespread shortages of the technology used in television sets, ended in 1945. As a result of a greatly reduced cost of materials as well as a sudden influx of workers seeking employment after the war, television-manufacturing companies multiplied. Competition kept the price of television sets modest, compared to the relatively high income of many U.S. households during the post-war years; by the end of the decade, the number of households with a television had increased more than a hundredfold.
>
> Identify in the table one *Cause* and one *Effect* of that cause that together, according to the author, likely contributed to the end of the Golden Age of Radio. Make only two selections, one in each column.

Cause	Effect	
O	O	An increase in competition among television manufacturers
O	O	A decrease in the number of U.S. homes with a radio
O	O	A widespread shortage of television-manufacturing technology
O	O	A reduction in the number of available manufacturing workers during World War II
O	O	A decrease in the cost of television-manufacturing materials
O	O	The relatively high income of post-war U.S. households

Step 1: Understand the Prompt and Question

The sentences signal a verbal- or logic-based problem. The fact that the question asks for a *Cause* and an *Effect* signals a CR-type verbal problem. Further, a cause-effect setup will usually need to be solved simultaneously.

The prompt first makes a general claim: The Golden Age of Radio ended in the 1950s when TV took over.

Then it provides a series of events that led to this outcome. After World War II ended in 1945, raw costs for making TVs went down a lot, and a lot of people were looking for work. In addition, household income was relatively high. These facts meant that companies could make a lot of TVs and sell them cheaply, allowing the number of households with TVs to greatly increase.

The blurb basically explains why TV was able to overtake radio as the entertainment medium of choice in the 1950s. The question asks what *Cause* led to what *Effect* that together contributed to the rise of TV.

Step 2: Plan Your Approach

The various facts in the argument are a bit jumbled together. Since the question asks specifically about a cause and an effect, it's worth the effort to map the information logically:

> WWII ends → workers avail + material costs decr.
> → more comp make more TVs
> → cheaper TVs
>
> Also: more inc to buy

There is one big chain of information: the business reasons that led to more cheap TVs on the market. Anything in the chain except for the last piece of information could be the cause, and anything in that chain except for the first piece of information could be the effect.

Separately, household income also increased, but the blurb doesn't provide any information as to why or how that happened. As a result, this fact can't be part of any cause-effect chain in the answers.

Step 3: Solve the Problem

Examine the answers, looking for a cause that falls earlier in the chain of events and an effect that both falls later in the chain of events and can reasonably be called a result of the earlier cause. Take a look at answer choice (A):

(A) *An increase in competition among television manufacturers*

This is in the chain, so it is one of the potential pieces of the puzzle, though it's not possible to say whether it's the cause or the effect without reviewing the rest of the answers. Put a star next to this information in your map. Now, move to choice (B):

(B) *A decrease in the number of U.S. homes with a radio*

This one is tricky. Technically, the blurb says only that *radio was supplanted by television*; it does not specify what this means. It could be that people who already had radios kept those radios but also bought TVs and spent more time watching TV. So the *number* of radios didn't necessarily have to decrease. Here is choice (C):

(C) *A widespread shortage of television-manufacturing technology*

The shortage existed during the war; once the war ended in 1945, these shortages no longer existed, and that fact contributed to the greater number of TVs built. This choice is the opposite of one cause of the growth of the TV market. Move on to choice (D):

(D) *A reduction in the number of available manufacturing workers during World War II*

It is true that fewer workers were available during the war but, as with the last choice, this changed after the war. The fact that more workers were available after the war helped the TV market to thrive. This choice is the opposite of one cause of the growth of the TV market. Here is choice (E):

(E) *A decrease in the cost of television-manufacturing materials*

This is part of the argument given in the blurb. First, the cost of these materials decreased. That allowed more companies to make TVs, and that in turn increased competition in the market, which is what the first answer choice said. This choice is the *cause* and the first answer is the *effect*. And finally, look at choice (F):

(F) *The relatively high income of post-war U.S. households*

This was also mentioned, but it is not connected to any other pieces of information in the blurb, so it cannot be either the cause or the effect.

The answers are:

Cause	Effect	
○	◉	An increase in competition among television manufacturers
○	○	A decrease in the number of U.S. homes with a radio
○	○	A widespread shortage of television-manufacturing technology
○	○	A reduction in the number of available manufacturing workers during World War II
◉	○	A decrease in the cost of television-manufacturing materials
○	○	The relatively high income of post-war U.S. households

UPS for Logic Two-Parts

The third category is the logic problem. This is a type of verbal-based reasoning with some more formalized analytical thinking.

Try this problem:

A chemical plant operating continuously has two 12-hour shifts, a day shift and a night shift, during each of which as many as five chemicals can be produced. Equipment limitations and safety regulations impose constraints on the types of chemicals that can be produced during the same shift. No more than two oxidizers can be produced per shift; the same limit holds true for monomers. On either shift, the sum of the safety rating for all chemicals should be no greater than 13 for health risk and 9 for reactivity.

Four chemicals have already been chosen for each shift, as shown below:

Day Shift

Acrylonitrile	(health = 4, reactivity = 2, oxidizer = no, monomer = yes)
Chloroprene	(health = 2, reactivity = 0, oxidizer = no, monomer = yes)
Hydrogen peroxide	(health = 3, reactivity = 2, oxidizer = yes, monomer = no)
Titanium dioxide	(health = 1, reactivity = 0, oxidizer = no, monomer = no)

Night Shift

Ammonium nitrate	(health = 2, reactivity = 3, oxidizer = yes, monomer = no)
Phosphine	(health = 4, reactivity = 2, oxidizer = no, monomer = no)
Potassium perchlorate	(health = 1, reactivity = 1, oxidizer = yes, monomer = no)
Propylene	(health = 1, reactivity = 1, oxidizer = no, monomer = yes)

Select a chemical that *Could* be added to either shift. Then, select a chemical that *Cannot* be added to either shift. Make only two selections, one in each column.

Could be added to either shift	Cannot be added to either shift	
○	○	Chlorine (health = 3, reactivity = 0, oxidizer = yes, monomer = no)
○	○	Ethylene (health = 3, reactivity = 2, oxidizer = no, monomer = yes)
○	○	Nickel carbonyl (health = 4, reactivity = 3, oxidizer = no, monomer = no)
○	○	Phenol (health = 3, reactivity = 0, oxidizer = no, monomer = no)
○	○	Sulfuric acid (health = 3, reactivity = 2, oxidizer = yes, monomer = no)
○	○	Vinyl chloride (health = 2, reactivity = 2, oxidizer = no, monomer = yes)

Step 1: Understand the Prompt and Question

Glance at the answers: text *and* numbers. The complexity of the information in the answers, coupled with the tables of information in the question stem, indicate that this is likely a logic problem.

This is also a really technical problem. Don't get caught up in the language. You don't need to know what a *monomer* is or what *reactivity* means. You just need to be able to classify things.

Whenever you have a logic problem, list out the details in a clear and organized way:

2 shifts: D and N
Max 5 chem per shift

Four of the five slots on each shift are already filled, so you're looking to fill the fifth slot. Map the constraints:

Slot constraints:
— No more than 2 O's per shift
— No more than 2 M's per shift
— H ≤ 13
— R ≤ 9

You have to identify a single chemical that *Could* fit either shift (there's only one) and another chemical that *Cannot* fit either shift (again, there's only one). The characteristics of the chemicals you are to choose from are in the answer choices.

Since you are going to have to work with the information from the answers in order to solve, jot down a little table on your scratch paper, something like this:

COULD	CANNOT	Chemical
		Chl
		Eth
		NC
		Ph
		SA
		VC

Use this to keep track of your eliminations as you go.

Step 2: Plan Your Approach

Since this problem is about following a chain of logic, first figure out what *must* and *must not* be true about the fifth chemical based on the given constraints and the four chemicals that are already set for each shift. Then, armed with these more refined constraints about the fifth possibility for each shift, go through the list of chemicals in the answer choices to figure out whether the chemical in question could be added to the shift.

7

Step 3: Solve the Problem

First, lay out what each shift already has:

Day Has:	Night Has:
H = 10	H = 8
R = 4	R = 7
1 O	2 O's
2 M's	1 M

You're only allowed 2 M's total, which the day shift has, and 2 O's total, which the night shift has. So the fifth chemical can't be an M or an O. Glance through the answers. In the COULD column, write NO for chlorine, ethylene, sulfuric acid, and vinyl chloride. Four down, two to go!

You're also allowed only 13 H total, and the day shift already has an H of 10, so the H rating of the final chemical has to be ≤ 3. Likewise, R can't be more than 9 total, and the night shift already has an R of 7, so the R rating of the final chemical has to be ≤ 2.

Scan the two remaining answers. Nickel carbonyl fails on both counts—it has an H rating of 4 and an R rating of 3.

The only chemical that *could* be added to either shift is phenol.

Use the work you've already done to figure out which chemical cannot go on either shift. Of the rejected answers, start with nickel carbonyl, since you've looked most carefully at that one so far and it has the highest health and reactivity safety ratings. As noted above, nickel carbonyl can't go on the day shift because it has an H rating of 4. And it can't go on the night shift because it has an R rating of 3. This is the one that cannot be added to either shift!

Here are the answers:

Could be added to either shift	Cannot be added to either shift	Chemical
○	○	Chlorine (health = 3, reactivity = 0, oxidizer = yes, monomer = no)
○	○	Ethylene (health = 3, reactivity = 2, oxidizer = no, monomer = yes)
○	◉	Nickel carbonyl (health = 4, reactivity = 3, oxidizer = no, monomer = no)
◉	○	Phenol (health = 3, reactivity = 0, oxidizer = no, monomer = no)
○	○	Sulfuric acid (health = 3, reactivity = 2, oxidizer = yes, monomer = no)
○	○	Vinyl chloride (health = 2, reactivity = 2, oxidizer = no, monomer = yes)

When you see a quant- or verbal-based Two-Part, it will usually resemble the questions in the Quant and Verbal sections of the exam, and you can use many of the same strategies you're learning for those sections. Unlike the more quant- and verbal-based Two-Parts, logic problems are different from what you are already learning for the rest of the test. Take a little time to understand the story and make an organized map of the given constraints. Use that map to make any logical inferences you can to narrow down the possibilities further.

Practice Your Skills

Now that you've learned about each problem type, take a look at the next chapter, which summarizes each type and provides some additional strategies for time management on IR. Then, log into Atlas to practice more Two-Parts—and all problem types.

Integrated Reasoning Strategies

In This Chapter

- Decision-Making on the GMAT

- Decision-Making on the EA

- How to Know When to Bail

- Table Analysis

- Graphics Interpretation

- Multi-Source Reasoning

- Two-Part Analysis

- When to Prioritize and When to Bail

In this chapter, you will review the Understand–Plan–Solve process and the specific strategies you learned for Tables, Graphs, MSRs, and Two-Parts. You will also learn how to optimize your test mindset and time management for the GMAT and the Executive Assessment.

CHAPTER 8 Integrated Reasoning Strategies

The four question types are identical on both the GMAT and the Executive Assessment (EA), so the solution process is the same no matter which test you take.

The sections work slightly differently on each test, though, so there are some differences in terms of your executive decision-making, depending upon which test you take.

Decision-Making on the GMAT

The section is 30 minutes long, and you'll need to solve a total of 12 problems. Unlike the Quant and Verbal sections, the Integrated Reasoning (IR) section is not adaptive; all 12 problems will be set before you start the section.

The vast majority of test-takers will not be able to address all 12 problems fully in that time, so plan to bail (guess *immediately*) on a number of problems in the section. (Also, if you are running low on time, just guess on every remaining problem. There are no penalties for wrong answers and you might get lucky!)

As on the Quant and Verbal sections, you must answer the current problem onscreen before you can move to the next one. In addition, as on Quant and Verbal, you cannot go back to a problem once you've answered it.

But that's okay! The test is constructed to allow you to get a number of problems wrong and still get a good score. Follow these guidelines depending upon your goal score:

If your goal score is...	Bail on this many problems	Per-problem time
6+	2	3 minutes
5	3	3 minutes 20 seconds
4	4	3 minutes 45 seconds

Decision-Making on the EA

The Integrated Reasoning section is 30 minutes long, and you'll need to solve a total of 12 problems. The section will come in two panels of 6 problems each.

Within one panel, you can move around as you choose among those six problems. When you finish the first panel and choose to move to the second panel, you will not be able to return to the first panel of problems.

Why do they do this? On the Executive Assessment, IR is section-adaptive (as are the Quant and Verbal sections). The first panel of six problems will be set in advance and will represent a range of difficulties. After you finish that panel, the test will give you a second panel of six problems that more closely targets the level at which you are performing, as illustrated below:

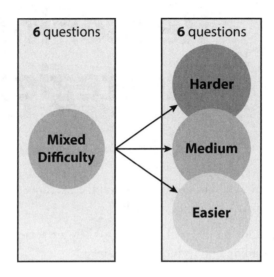

Further, your IR performance will determine your starting points for the Verbal and Quant sections, as illustrated below:

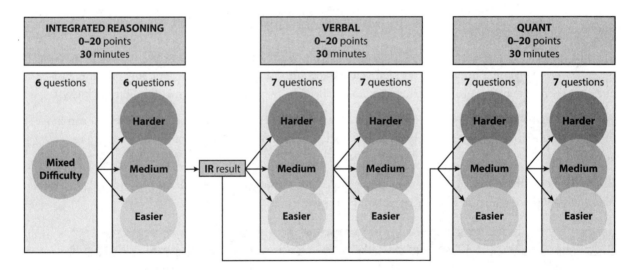

The vast majority of test-takers will not be able to fully complete all 12 IR problems in the 30 minutes provided, so plan to bail—guess immediately—on at least one problem in each panel. Because you can move around among the 6 problems in one panel, this decision is easier than it is on the GMAT. (Also, do answer everything. There are no penalties for incorrect answers and you might get lucky!)

Plan to use half of your time, 15 minutes, on the first panel. If you bail on one problem, that gives you 3 minutes for each of the remaining problems. If you decide to bail on a second one, you'll have 3 minutes and 45 seconds per problem on the four that you do answer.

In general, plan to bail on one problem in each panel and then give yourself one more "freebie" on top of that. You can choose whether to use the freebie in the first or second panel.

Move through each panel twice. The first time, solve the problems that seem straightforward to you. Mark the others with a flag as you go; these are your bail candidates. Once you've finished the ones that you find easier, scroll through the flagged problems to decide where you want to bail and what else you want to try.

How to Know When to Bail

First, a bail is a problem on which you guess immediately so that you save that time to use elsewhere. If you try a problem but can't find the answer, still guess on that problem—but don't count it as one of your bail problems.

Before test day (practice or the real thing!), take stock of your strengths and weaknesses. A low-ROI (return on investment) problem is one that combines both a topic area that you don't like and a weaker problem type for you. Know how to recognize these low-ROI questions quickly, so that you can get out right away when you see them.

Ask yourself some questions to help determine what to do and what *not* to do:

- Generally better at Quant or at Verbal?
- Comfortable with tables and/or graphs? (Do Table and/or Graph problems.)
- Good at piecing together information from different sources? (Then Multi-Source Reasoning is for you.)
- Comfortable with standard Critical Reasoning (CR) and/or Quant multiple-choice? (Look for these opportunities on Two-Part problems.)

When you finish a practice test, first review the section globally. Are you happy with the decisions that you made about where to invest time and effort and where *not* to? In hindsight, you might realize that you cut off one problem too quickly. What clues can help you to know next time that you actually can do this problem?

You may also realize that you spent too much time on another problem that you really had no idea how to do. Likewise, what are the clues that you want to spot next time so that you know to bail—guess and move on—right away?

Work out your decision-making processes before test day so that you can react appropriately to different scenarios on test day.

The four IR problem types are summarized on the following pages.

Table Analysis

Key details:

- Main feature: Table
- Type of problem: One Either-Or question
- Key Strategy: SEE (Sort, Eyeball, Estimate)

Table prompts will, of course, contain a table, along with one either-or question (e.g., true/false, yes/no). You'll answer three statements, each one of which must be answered correctly in order to earn credit on that problem.

The table may also be accompanied by a blurb: a separate paragraph of text that describes the information in the table and may even provide additional information you'll need to answer the question.

Before starting to solve the problem, glance through the three statements. If at least two look okay to you, go ahead and solve this problem. Even if you have to guess on one statement, you'll have a 50/50 chance if you were able to do the other two statements correctly.

If two or all three statements look hard enough that you're not sure you can do them or think they'll take too long, consider bailing on this problem.

Step 1: Understand the Prompt and Question

Glance at the title (if applicable), column headers, and rows. Read the blurb and examine the data in the table, thinking about the *what* and *so what*. What types of information do the different rows and columns contain? What connections (if any) exist between the columns? If appropriate, jot down a note or two.

Once you understand the basics, glance at the data in the table. Are there any surprising data points (e.g., some entries of 0 or some entries that are very different from the others)? Don't try to figure out why these entries are what they are; just notice them and keep them in mind for later.

You'll have one either-or question. Glance at all three statements before you read the question itself. Are they connected or unrelated? If connected, you can solve them simultaneously.

Next, read the question stem and jot down anything that will help keep you focused on what you need to do. If you don't understand what the question is asking you to do, guess and move on.

Step 2: Plan Your Approach

If you can solve some or all of the statements simultaneously, figure out which pieces you can solve together and in what order you want to tackle them.

If you are solving separately, start with whichever statement seems easiest to you. If they're all about the same, go in order. Use the SEE (sort, eyeball, estimate) strategy to guide your thinking.

For the first statement you tackle, how should you sort the table to make your job easier?

Can you eyeball any of the data—see what the trend is without calculating anything at all? If you do have to calculate anything, can you estimate at any point along the way? How heavily?

Step 3: Solve the Problem

Dive in! Sort the table and examine the data. Wherever you can, eyeball and estimate. If you have to perform a calculation, make sure to do so on your scrap paper, not in your head. You do have a calculator if you need a precise answer; write down the calculation you want to do before you plug it into the calculator. (But don't perform a precise calculation unless you really need to.)

If you get stuck, think about whether a different table sort might get you unstuck.

Finally, repeat the process for the other two statements.

Graphics Interpretation

Key details:

- Main feature: Graph, diagram or visual of some sort
- Content: Can be standard math or analytical
- Type of problem: One Fill-in-the-Blank question
- Key Strategy: SEE (Select, Eyeball, Estimate)

Graphs may consist of a standard math graph, a chart, a timeline, or even a geometry diagram. Anything is possible, but if you're given something nonstandard, you will also be given instructions as to how to read the graph.

The graph may also be accompanied by a blurb that describes the visual and may even provide additional information you'll need to solve the problem.

The question will consist of one or two sentences with a total of two blanks with drop-down menus for the answers. You may be given anywhere from three to six multiple-choice options for each blank.

If one of the two blanks looks too hard to answer, check how many answer choices it has. If it has only three or four and you can answer the other blank, then you'll still have pretty decent odds to make a lucky guess. If, on the other hand, that blank has five or six answer choices, you might want to bail on the entire problem.

Step 1: Understand the Prompt and Question

First, glance at the visual—is it a type of graph you recognize or something unusual? Then, take the first step of SEE (select, eyeball, estimate). Click on each drop-down menu (where you see the word *Select*) to see the answer choice options. Words? Numbers? If numbers, how spread out are they?

Next, read the title and blurb (if present) to orient you to the information given in the graph. Then, examine the graph, thinking about the *what* and *so what*. What types of information does it contain? What does each point, line, bar, box, arrow, or other visual represent?

If the graph type is completely unfamiliar to you, take a little more time to orient yourself. Jot down anything that will help you to remember the big picture. If you've read through the blurb and examined the graph carefully but still find yourself lost, guess and move on.

Once you understand the basics, glance at the data in the graph. Are there any surprising data points (e.g., some entries or parts that are very different from others)? Don't try to figure out why these entries are what they are; just notice them and keep them in mind for later.

Next, read the question stem and jot down anything that you may find useful. Then, click on the first blank to show the possible answer choices and read through the first part of the text that applies to that blank. When appropriate, click on the second blank to see those options.

Do not read the statement without looking at the multiple-choice options! The options may completely change the way you plan for and solve the problem. For instance, if the answers are values that are spread apart, you'll know you can estimate. Alternatively, you may have been expecting specific values but the blank actually contains qualifiers such as *greater than* and *less than*, allowing you to compare (either to a benchmark value or an estimate) rather than calculate.

The two blanks may be related, in which case you will solve simultaneously, or the two blanks may be independent. Know the relationship between the blanks before you start to solve.

Step 2: Plan Your Approach

Which blank is easier to answer first? Start there.

Which parts of the graph do you need in order to tackle your starting blank? You may need just one or two of the data points or one portion of the diagram given.

Do you just need to find or identify something, or will you need to perform a calculation? Can you eyeball or estimate values, or do you need to be more precise?

Step 3: Solve the Problem

Again, make sure that you are solving in a form that matches the drop-down answers given. Do any calculations on your scratch paper, and don't hesitate to pop up the calculator when needed. As always, write out the calculation you want to perform before plugging it into your calculator.

Wherever you can save time and effort by eyeballing or estimating, do so!

Multi-Source Reasoning

Key details:

- Main feature: Two or three tabs
- Types of problems: Typically three problems (though can be two or four)
    - 1 standard multiple-choice
    - 2 either-or problems

Multi-Source Reasoning (MSR) prompts contain two or three tabs of information and are typically accompanied by three separate problems. One of the problems is usually in standard multiple-choice format, while the other two are typically in either-or form (e.g., true/false, yes/no). On either-or problems, each of the three statements must be answered correctly in order to earn credit on that problem.

You'll need some additional time up front to process all of the MSR text, but this time is spread across the three problems you'll solve. Expect to spend about two to three minutes orienting yourself to everything in the tabs, then to spend about two additional minutes per problem.

On the Executive Assessment, a set of MSR problems will always appear together in one panel. Scroll through all three problems and do whichever one seems easiest first. It's generally not a good idea to decide to bail on the entire set of three, since they will appear in a single panel—missing three out of six would likely drop your score too low—but you could choose to bail on one of the three.

On the GMAT, you could choose to bail on all three MSRs. Just note that you can't view all three problems before deciding whether to bail—you'll have to decide what to do about the first problem before you can see the second. Glance at the problem itself before you try to process the information in the tabs. If it looks really hard, you might decide to bail on that immediately. In this case, guess randomly and move to the second question (still without looking at the tabs). If you also want to bail on the second problem, then bail on the entire MSR problem set; it's not worth it to learn the tabs if you're only going to do one problem. If you think you can answer the second problem, then dive into the tabs to learn the information.

Step 1: Understand the Prompt and Question

Glance at the tab titles for a hint of the topics covered. Use the titles to help you start creating your Multi-Source Reasoning map.

Dive into the first tab. As you read, create a map: Jot down high-level information on your scrap paper to help you figure out where to go when you get to the questions.

As you work your way through the tabs, think about the *what* and the *so what*: What does the tab say and what are the implications of that information? If a tab contains a table, diagram, or other visual, note that in your map. (Reminder: Tables in MSR tabs are *not* sortable.)

After you've looked at all of the tabs, take a moment to think about how they interconnect. You might even click through them all again to remind yourself.

MSRs come with two different kinds of questions: standard multiple-choice and either-or. Answer standard multiple-choice questions in the same way that you would answer a Reading Comprehension or quant problem. For either-or problems, use the same process you learned for Tables.

8

Step 2: Plan Your Approach

Which tabs are you likely to need in order to address this statement? What information do you need to review in those tabs? Reread the relevant information, jotting down notes if appropriate.

Will you need to do math? On multiple-choice questions, you can use the same strategies you learn for the Quant section of the exam: Smart Numbers, Work Backwards, Test Cases, and so on. Math-focused either-or statements can sometimes be solved in a similar way; if this is the case, take some time to figure out how to organize your scratch paper. Then you'll be able to run all three statements through the same process. (And don't forget to estimate wherever possible!)

On either-or questions, if you can solve some or all of the statements simultaneously, figure out which pieces you can solve together and in what order you want to tackle them.

Verbal- or logic-focused multiple-choice questions can be solved similarly to Reading Comprehension problems: Identify the source material you need to review, reread that material, formulate your own answer to the question, and look through the answer choices for a match.

Step 3: Solve the Problem

Finally, follow your plan! Don't hesitate to go back into the tabs to check or recheck any information you need. Multi-Source Reasoning is like an open-book test: The material is always in front of you. Take advantage of that fact, especially since there is so much information; don't just rely on your memory.

Two-Part Analysis

> Key details:
>
> - Main feature: Five or six answer choices displayed in a table at the bottom
> - Content: Can be quant-, verbal-, or logic-based
> - Type of problem: Two-Part multiple-choice
> - Key Strategies: Same as for Quant and Verbal sections of exam

Two-Parts typically fall into one of three categories: quant, verbal, or logic. Quant-based Two-Parts will look very much like standard Problem Solving problems, and verbal-based Two-Parts will typically resemble Critical Reasoning problems. The logic variety doesn't show up elsewhere on the GMAT.

You'll choose from among the *same* five or six answers for each of the two parts of the question. Sometimes, the two parts will be connected and you'll solve for both simultaneously; other times, they'll be independent and you'll solve separately.

Step 1: Understand the Prompt and Question

Start by glancing at the answer choices. Do you have numbers? Words? Sentences? That will give you a quick idea of whether you have a quant-based question or whether it's verbal or logic.

Next, glance at the question stem (not the whole big paragraph—just the question stem after that). What is the question asking you to do?

Quant-based:	Asks you to calculate something
	Contains numbers, formulas, or similar
	May ask you to calculate connected values (such as an *x* and *y* that simultaneously make an equation true)
Verbal-based:	May ask you a Critical Reasoning–type question (strengthen, weaken, find an assumption)
	May ask you a connected question (such as cause and effect)
Logic-based:	Asks you to complete some kind of scenario
	May contain tables of information or lists of rules or constraints to follow

Now, read through the actual prompt and then reread the question stem. As always, jot down notes as you read to help orient yourself to the information.

Step 2: Plan Your Approach

For quant-based and verbal-based problems, you can use the same strategies that you use in the Quant and Verbal sections of the exam. If you need to solve the two parts simultaneously, figure out how to set up that solution or reasoning method before you start to solve.

For logic-based problems, you're essentially going to reason your way to the answer. First, use any constraints given in the prompt to narrow down the possibilities of whatever scenario you've been given. Do this narrowing *before* you dive into the main solution process.

Step 3: Solve the Problem

For quant- and verbal-based problems, use your standard solving techniques. For logic problems, take your narrowed-down constraints and play out the possible scenarios with the goal of eliminating incorrect answers. Most of the time, you can work from the answer choices, testing each one.

When to Prioritize and When to Bail

What are your IR strengths and weaknesses?

You may already have a good idea. If not, see how things go on your next practice exam. When you're done, analyze those problems and categorize into one of three buckets:

1. Bucket 1 Strengths: I can get these right and I don't need extra time to do them.

2. Bucket 2 Opportunities: I can learn to do this—correctly or faster or both. This is where I'll concentrate my practice until my next practice test.

3. Bucket 3 Bails: If I see something like this on my next practice test, I'm going to guess immediately and move on. (Later on, I might decide to study some of these—but not between now and my next practice test.)

Focus on Bucket 2

Your bucket 2 items (i.e., Opportunities) are your priorities for the next few weeks (or until your next practice exam). Maybe you got the problem right but took too long to do so. In that case, your focus will be on learning how to do that type of task more efficiently in future.

If you made a careless mistake, dig in to understand precisely *what* mistake you made and *why* you made it. Then, figure out what new habit you can implement that will minimize the chances of that type of mistake in the future. Finally, practice that new habit enough to make it your default process.

Sometimes, you will have missed the problem legitimately—you really didn't know how to do it—but when you review the solution, you feel comfortable learning this material. In that case, go for it!

Don't Focus on Bucket 3—for Now

You can't possibly study *everything* between now and your next practice test. There aren't enough hours in the day. Spend your precious study time on areas that are the most likely to pay off—and that doesn't include problems you took way too long to do and got wrong anyway. Likewise, when the official solution makes no sense to you, don't prioritize learning how to do that problem.

After your next practice test, you might return to some of your bucket 3 problem types or topic areas and realize that you feel more comfortable with them. At that point, you can move them up to bucket 2.

Or, you might still hate them! If so, leave them in bucket 3. By the time you get to the real test, the problem types or content areas still sitting in bucket 3 will be your bail problems. Then, you'll review how to recognize quickly that a particular problem is in this bail category so that you can guess right away during the test, saving you valuable time and mental energy for other problems.

How to Write Better Sentences

In This Appendix

- Structure Your Sentences—Then Flesh Them Out

- Pay Attention to Grammar (to a Degree)

- Choose Your Words—and Vary Them

In this appendix, you will learn how to write complex sentences in a clear and cogent manner.

APPENDIX A How to Write Better Sentences

Only the GMAT has an Essay section, but even if you're taking the Executive Assessment, why not learn how to make your sentences better in general? For one thing, your efforts will pay off on the rest of the exam, whether GMAT or EA: The more you understand about sentence construction, the better you'll be able to read on test day. And every part of the exam demands that you read sentences quickly and effectively.

By the way, if you're a non-native-English speaker, GMAC says that "in considering the elements of standard written English, readers are trained to be sensitive and fair in evaluating the responses of examinees whose first language is not English." In other words, you'll get a little consideration. Your language still needs to be intelligible, but they're not going to penalize you for messing up a few idioms.

Structure Your Sentences—Then Flesh Them Out

A sentence should represent a thought. Thus, the core structure of the sentence should represent the skeleton of that thought, stripped of all flesh.

To analyze a sentence quickly, break it into **Topic** and **Comment**:

>   Topic: what you're talking about

>   Comment: what you're saying about the topic

Here's a possible first sentence for the response to an essay question:

>   While the author makes several valid points, her conclusion that regular exercise has no benefits for losing weight fails to account for several factors that would serve to undermine that conclusion.

Strip that sentence down to its essentials to find the topic–comment structure:

Her conclusion . . .	fails to account for several factors.
Topic	*Comment*
"What are you talking about?"	"What are you saying about that conclusion?"

Good sentences have obvious—and intentional—core structures.

Now, how do you expand upon the core? How do you put flesh on the bones? You have many options.

1. Make Compounds with *and*, *or*, and Other Connecting Words

You can use these words to add a compound structure to the sentence. Here is a compound verb:

>   The argument fails to account for several factors and makes unwarranted assumptions.

2. Add Modifiers to Describe Parts of the Sentence

The simplest modifiers are single words (adjectives, adverbs, and possessives):

The *author's* conclusion *completely* fails to account for several *important* factors.

Modifiers answer questions about parts of the sentence: *Whose* argument? *What kinds* of concerns? *To what degree* does the argument omit concerns?

Here is an example of a more complex modifier:

The conclusion *that the author draws* fails to account for several factors *that must be addressed.*

Modifiers are a great way to lengthen and enrich sentences. To add modifiers, ask questions of the parts you already have in place:

What kind of points?	several valid points
Which conclusion?	that regular exercise has no benefits for losing weight
What would the factors do?	serve to undermine that conclusion

3. Add Sentence-Level Subordinate Clauses

Words such as *because, since, if, while,* and *although* indicate logical connections between your thoughts:

While the author makes valid points, her conclusion . . . fails to account for several factors.

The author acknowledges that the argument isn't completely terrible but still asserts that it is flawed.

You can also use a semicolon to join two sentences, adding a relational word such as *therefore* or *moreover:*

Her conclusion fails to account for several factors; *moreover, it downplays the importance of two relevant pieces of evidence.*

As you use all these tools, experimenting with lengthening sentences, you might find yourself going too far. Don't add just to add; make every word count.

If you have a cumbersome sentence, first try breaking it into more than one sentence. If that doesn't work, move the heavy stuff to the end. Shift the grammatical core up front, so that a reader doesn't have to wade through a whole lot of modifiers to understand the gist of what the sentence is saying.

Pay Attention to Grammar (to a Degree)

You need to know grammatical rules for Sentence Correction; you might as well apply this knowledge to sentence *construction,* too. Yes, you can make occasional mistakes with grammar in your writing; they aren't expecting a perfect essay. And remember that the essay scoring rewards volume. If you have a choice between writing a new sentence and polishing another sentence's grammar, you should generally write the new sentence.

All that said, the better your grammar, the clearer your thoughts. Pay attention to the following issues.

Parallelism: When you use parallel markers, make the parts logically and structurally parallel:

X and Y   X, Y, and Z   both X and Y   X or Y   not only X but also Y

For example:

> Her conclusion not only omits certain studies but also downplays the importance of evidence that she does cite.

Pronouns: The Deadly Five pronouns—*it, its, they, them,* and *their*—can cause serious problems in writing. Try to ensure that these words have clear, meaningful antecedents—the nouns that they refer to. For example:

Sloppy: If cars go too fast on the highway, it can cause crashes.

What does *it* refer to? The highway?

Better: If cars go too fast on the highway, crashes can occur.

          Cars that go too fast on the highway can cause crashes.

          Highway speeding can cause crashes.

Modifiers: Put modifiers next to the thing you want to modify.

Your essay does not have to exhibit perfect grammar to get a great score, let alone a decent score. Even 6.0 essays can have minor grammatical flaws. And you don't need a 6.0 anyway!

By the way, feel free to use the passive voice. For one thing, it's grammatically correct. More important, the passive voice in English provides a useful way of flipping sentences around so that you can control the topic–comment structure as you desire. Both of the sentences below are correct:

> Highway speeding can cause crashes.

> Crashes can be caused by highway speeding.

Choose Your Words—and Vary Them

Words are like notes on a piano. Play them and play around with them to appreciate their resonance. For the essay, it's worth distinguishing two categories of words: signal words and substance words.

Signal Words indicate relationships to previous text. Signals are super-handy as you *read* academic text (e.g., passages in Reading Comprehension). The same words are also super-handy as you *write* that kind of text. Don't be afraid to tell your readers exactly where they are and what's happening. Here are some good signal words to use in your writing:

Relationship	Signal
Focus attention	As for, Regarding, In reference to
Add to previous point	Furthermore, Moreover, In addition, As well as, Also, Likewise, Too
Provide contrast	On one hand/On the other hand, While, Rather, Instead, In contrast, Alternatively
Provide conceding contrast (author unwillingly agrees)	Granted, It is true that, Certainly, Admittedly, Despite, Although
Provide emphatic contrast (author asserts own position)	But, However, Even so, All the same, Still, That said, Nevertheless, Nonetheless, Yet, Otherwise, Despite [concession], [assertion]

Relationship	Signal
Dismiss previous point	In any event, In any case
Point out similarity	Likewise, In the same way
Structure the discussion	First, Second, etc., To begin with, Next, Finally, Again
Give example	For example, In particular, For instance
Generalize	In general, To a great extent, Broadly speaking
Sum up, perhaps with exception	In conclusion, In brief, Overall, Except for, Besides
Indicate logical result	Therefore, Thus, As a result, So, Accordingly, Hence
Indicate logical cause	Because, Since, As, Resulting from
Restate for clarity	In other words, That is, Namely, So to speak
Hedge or soften position	Apparently, At least, Can, Could, May, Might, Should, Possibly, Likely
Strengthen position	After all, Must, Have to, Always, Never, etc.
Introduce surprise	Actually, In fact, Indeed
Reveal author's attitude	Fortunately, Unfortunately, So-called, *Other adverbs*

Substance Words contain real content. Our main suggestion here is to have a mini thesaurus up your sleeve for certain ideas that you are likely to express—and re-express—*no matter what particular essay you must write.* For instance, you will need to have more than one way of making this point: "The argument is flawed."

Simply memorizing a list of synonyms and spitting them back out will do you little good. The 2.0 (*Seriously Flawed*) essay published in the *Official Guide* is riddled with these terms, seemingly as a substitute for thought. But you don't want to spend a lot of time searching for another way to say that an argument is flawed. Use these lists to free your mind up to do real thinking:

Argument is good:	sound, persuasive, thorough, convincing, logical, compelling, credible, effective
Perfect:	airtight, watertight
Argument is bad:	flawed (of course!), defective, imperfect, faulty, fallacious, unpersuasive, unconvincing, ineffective; it overgeneralizes, makes an extreme claim, takes an unsupported logical leap, makes an unwarranted assumption, fails to justify X or prove Y or address Z
Really bad:	unsound, illogical, specious, erroneous, invalid, unfounded, baseless
Maliciously bad:	misleading, deceptive
Flaw:	defect, omission, fault, error, failing, imperfection, concern, issue, area, aspect, feature to be addressed, opportunity for improvement

Assess an argument:	judge, evaluate, critique, examine, scrutinize, weigh
Strengthen an argument:	support, bolster, substantiate, reinforce, improve, fortify, justify, address concerns, fix issues, reduce or eliminate defects, prove
Weaken an argument:	undermine, damage, harm, water down, impair, remove support for, disprove, destroy, demolish, annihilate, obliterate

Practice using some of these words in your emails or work documents. Don't go too wild—no word is precisely interchangeable with any other. Pick one word a day from the list above and find a way to use it. Keep an eye out for its use in print so that you learn the word's strength, spin, and tonal qualities.

In your essay, avoid slang and jargon. You risk confusing or even offending your readers. You don't have to stick to highly formal registers of English; feel free to use contractions (such as *don't*) and short, concrete words (such as *stick to*). However, only write what's appropriate for an academic paper.

APPENDIX B
Quantitative Topics

In This Appendix

- Decimals, Percents, and Ratios

- Statistics

In this appendix, you will learn about certain quant topics that are commonly tested on the Integrated Reasoning section of the GMAT and the Executive Assessment. Additional material on these and other topics can be found in Manhattan Prep's *GMAT All the Quant* guide.

APPENDIX B Quantitative Topics

Decimals, Percents, and Ratios

If you are not already very comfortable with solving percent and decimal problems, review core GMAT and EA Quant section materials, such as the Manhattan Prep *GMAT All the Quant* guide. (The Quant section of both exams tests the same material and has the same question types.) This section describes only the new wrinkles that Integrated Reasoning adds to these sorts of problems.

Here are the key differences in how the exam sections treat these topics:

Integrated Reasoning	Quant
Decimals and percents are encountered more often than fractions. Ratios are also important. *Example:* Which of the following stocks has the highest price-to-earnings ratio?	Fractions are as common as the others. *Example:* $$\frac{1}{3x} + \frac{3}{4 + \frac{2}{x}} = ?$$
Percent problems draw on real data in graph, chart, and paragraph form. *Example:* Was the percent increase in imports from China to the U.S. greater than the percent increase in imports from Brazil to the U.S.?	Percent problems can be more abstract. *Example:* If x is $y\%$ of z, what is $y\%$ of x in terms of z?

For both Quant and IR, you need to know standard percent formulas, such as the percent change formula: $\frac{\text{Change}}{\text{Original}} \times 100\% = \%$ Change. Be ready to compute percent increases and decreases using the calculator. For example, if you need to increase 107.5 by 17%, you will need to multiply 107.5 by 1.17, so punch the following into your calculator:

$$\boxed{1}\,\boxed{0}\,\boxed{7}\,\boxed{.}\,\boxed{5}\,\boxed{\times}\,\boxed{1}\,\boxed{.}\,\boxed{1}\,\boxed{7}\,\boxed{=}$$

The result is 125.775.

How does this compare to the result of increasing 105.5 by 19%? Don't look for an estimation shortcut (slightly greater increase to a slightly smaller number—tough call). Just punch it in and see. The result is 125.545, so this calculated number is slightly less than the first one.

Common Percent Question Traps

Here are four percent traps that you are likely to see on the IR section:

1. **Percents vs. Quantities.** Some numbers are percents. Others are quantities. Don't mistake one for the other, especially when numbers are embedded in text:

   > If a carrot has a higher percentage of vitamin A relative to its total vitamin composition than a mango does, does the carrot have more vitamin A than the mango does?

   It's impossible to tell because you don't know the total vitamin content of either the carrot or the mango. Perhaps carrots have a lot lower vitamin content overall than mangoes do. A big fraction of a small whole could possibly be less (in milligrams, say) than a smaller fraction of a bigger whole.

2. **Percent of what.** Don't assume that all of the percents given are percents of the same total. Some of the percents given may well be percents of something *other* than the grand total. If you miss that little detail, you will get the answer wrong:

   > If 60% of customers at the produce stand purchased fruit and 20% of fruit purchasers purchased bananas, what percent of customers did not purchase bananas?

   A casual reader might see *20%...purchased bananas* and decide that the answer must be 80%. However, the problem says that 20% *of fruit purchasers* purchased bananas. Fruit purchasers are a subset of the total—only 60%. The banana-buying percent of *all* customers is just $0.60 \times 0.20 = 0.12$, or 12%. The answer is 100% – 12%, which is equal to 88%, not 80%.

3. **Percent *of* vs. percent *greater than*.** Try the following two questions:

   1. 10 is what percent of 8?
   2. 10 is what percent greater than 8?

   The first question asks for the percent *of*. The answer is $\frac{10}{8}$, or 125%.

   The second question asks for a percent *change*. The answer is $\frac{10 - 8}{8}$, or 25%.

   The wording is very similar. Pay attention to the details!

3. **Percent decrease and then increase. Consider this question:**

   > If the price of lettuce is decreased by 20% and then the reduced price is increased by 22%, is the resulting final price less than, equal to, or greater than the original price?

   The resulting final price is less than the original price, not equal to it or greater than it. In fact, if you first decrease the price by 20%, you would have to increase the reduced price by 25% to get back to the original price.

   Plug in a number to see for yourself. If you decrease $100 by 20%, you'll have $80.

   You would have to increase $80 by $20 in order to get back to $100. Because $20 is 25% of $80, you would have to increase the price by 25%. Increasing $80 by 22% yields $97.60, which is less than $100.

Statistics

Statistics topics are important on Integrated Reasoning, since IR is all about analyzing real-world data.

Integrated Reasoning	Quant
Real-world statistical terms, including regression and correlation, are used to describe realistic data presented in tables and charts.	Statistics terms, such as *mean* and *median*, are used primarily to create tricky problems based on contrived data, such as sets of consecutive integers.
Example: The mean age of the participants in the marketing study is 24.	*Example:* How much greater than the mean is the median of the set of integers n, $n + 2$, $n + 4$, and $n + 6$?

When you have a lot of quantitative information, statistics can help boil it down to a few key numbers so that you can make good probabilistic predictions and better decisions.

This section covers essentially every statistics concept you need for IR. Most of the statistics problems on the IR section just require that you understand certain definitions.

Descriptive Statistics

Say there are 320 consultants at your company, all of whom graduated from business school, and you want to think about the *number of years* since each one graduated.

To make things simple, you'll probably round to the nearest whole number (instead of having data like 5.25 years, 7.8 years, etc.). Whole numbers are *discrete* (or able to be separated and counted), so with this information, you can make a *histogram* to display the count in each category. For example:

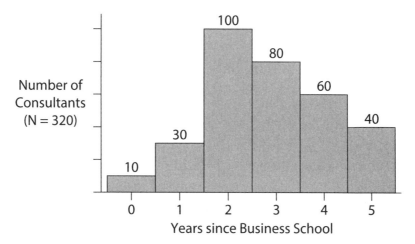

These three terms are very commonly tested on both IR and Quant:

1. Average (arithmetic mean)

2. Median

3. Mode

The **Average** (or **Arithmetic Mean**) is the most important. You may already know the formula from the Quant section:

$$\text{Mean} = \frac{\text{Sum of all terms}}{\text{Number of terms}}$$

Add up everyone's *Years since Business School*, and divide that total by 320, the number of consultants at the company:

$$
\begin{aligned}
\text{Mean years} &= \frac{\text{Total years}}{\text{Number of consultants}} \\
&= \frac{(10 \times 0) + (30 \times 1) + (100 \times 2) + (80 \times 3) + (60 \times 4) + (40 \times 5)}{320} \\
&= \frac{0 + 30 + 200 + 240 + 240 + 200}{320} \\
&= \frac{910}{320} \\
\text{Mean years} &= 2.84375
\end{aligned}
$$

The **Median** is the middle number, or the 50th percentile: Half of the people have more years since business school (or the same number) and half have fewer years (or the same number).

If you have an odd number of terms, say {101, 102, 103, 104, 105}, then the median is the middle number (in this case, 103). If you have an even number of terms, say {201, 202, 203, 204}, then the median is the average of the two middle terms (in this case, 202.5). In the earlier example, the median of the *Years since Business School* distribution is 3 years because both the 160th consultant and the 161st consultant are 3 years out of business school.

The **Mode** is the observation that shows up the most often, corresponding to the highest column on the histogram. The histogram for the consultants peaks at the 2-year bar, so the mode is 2 years since business school.

The Spread

Mean, median, and mode are all *central* measures—they answer the question, *Where's the center of all the data?* However, you often need to know how spread out the data is.

The crudest measure of spread is **Range**, which is just the largest value minus the smallest value. While range is easy to calculate, it's susceptible to **Outliers**—oddball observations that, rightly or wrongly, lie far away from most of the others. For example, if one person in your program is in her 70s and has been out of school for 50 years, then your range of *Years since College* would be huge because of that one outlier.

A better measure of spread is **Standard Deviation**. You will never have to calculate standard deviation on the exam because it is such a pain to do so without Excel or other software.

Roughly, standard deviation indicates how far, on average, each data point is from the mean. That's not the precise mathematical definition, but it's close enough for the exam.

For example, if your data points are {3, 3, 3, 3, 3}, then the standard deviation is 0, because every data point is 0 units away from the average of the set. If your data points are {1, 2, 3, 4, 5}, then your standard deviation is something greater than 0 (remember, you won't have to calculate it), because only one of the data points equals the average; the other four are more spread out. For example:

Which data set has the higher standard deviation: {1, 2, 3, 4, 5} or {10, 20, 30, 40, 50}?

In the first data set, the numbers are very close to the mean of 3. In the second, the numbers are much farther away, on average, from the mean of 30. The second set has the higher standard deviation.

Standard deviation is incredibly important in finance, operations, and other subjects. For now, focus on an intuitive understanding. For instance, if you add outliers, the standard deviation increases. If you remove outliers, it decreases. If you just shift every number up by some constant value, the standard deviation stays the same.

Correlation

Up to now, everything has had to do with one variable—one measurement. For example, imagine that you were given data on the number of years since someone graduated from college:

Person	Years since college
You	4
Anika Atwater	2.5
Bao Yang	6
. . .	. . .

What if you get *two* pieces of data about each person? Now you can look at more interesting patterns:

Person	Years since college	Height
You	4	5 feet 7 inches
Anika Atwater	2.5	5 feet 10 inches
Bao Yang	6	5 feet 2 inches
. . .	. . .	. . .

To find a pattern, put all of these observations on a scatterplot:

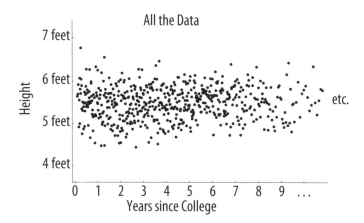

The disorganized jumble of data points shows that the two variables, *Years since College* and *Height*, are basically **Uncorrelated**. Numbers are correlated when they increase together or decrease together; in this case, there is **No Correlation** because no such pattern exists.

In contrast, if you plot *Years since College* versus *Age*, you'll get a pattern. Typically, older people have been out of college longer:

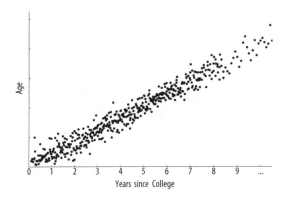

Most people are either high on both scales or low on both scales. This means that *Years since College* and *Age* are highly correlated. That is, there is a **Positive Correlation** between the two variables.

If the data is presented to you in a table, you'll have to sort by one of the two parameters and then compare the two columns. If the numbers mostly increase (or decrease) together, then there is a positive correlation. If one increases while the other decreases, the two have a negative correlation. If no such pattern exists, the two metrics have no correlation. To summarize:

Correlation	Pattern	Example
Positive	Points cluster around a line of positive slope	

Correlation	Pattern	Example
None	No pattern (jumble) or a nonlinear pattern	
Negative	Points cluster around a line of negative slope	

Regression

If you're asked to do a linear regression, you have to find the **Best-Fit Line**, or **Regression Line**, through a scatterplot. With such a line, you can describe the relationship between x and y more precisely and even predict values of y from values of x:

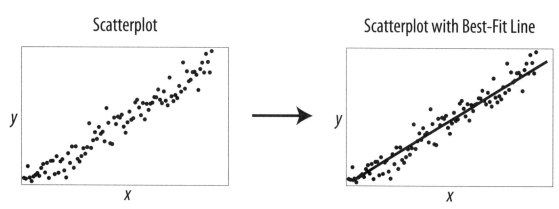

Scatterplot → Scatterplot with Best-Fit Line

The best-fit regression line minimizes the distance, in some sense, between the points and the line. You can see this intuitively:

Terrible fit

Better fit

Best fit

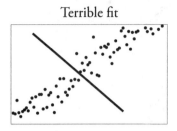
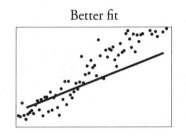
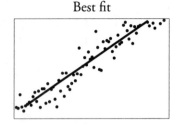

The exam will never ask you to compute a linear regression, but a graphical Integrated Reasoning problem might ask about the slope of a regression line:

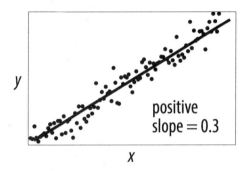

If the two variables are positively correlated, then the regression line will have positive slope (as one variable increases, so does the other one). Likewise, if the two variables are negatively correlated, the regression line will have negative slope (as one variable increases, the other decreases).

Remember that to find a line is to find its equation. The general equation of a line is $y = mx + b$. The letter m represents the **Slope** of the line, while b represents the ***y*-intercept**, where the line crosses the *y*-axis:

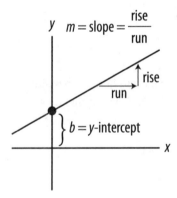

A line with the equation $y = 3x - 2$ intercepts the y-axis at $(0, -2)$. On this line, if x increases by 1, y increases by 3:

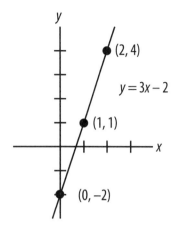

Finding the line means finding the values for the slope m and the y-intercept b.

Go beyond books.
Try us for free.

In-Person

Find a GMAT course near you and attend the first session free, no strings attached.

Online

Enjoy the flexibility of prepping from home or the office with our online course.

On-Demand

Prep where you are, when you want with GMAT Interact™ – our on-demand course.

Try our classes and on-demand products for free at manhattanprep.com/gmat.

Not sure which is right for you? Try all three! Or give us a call and we'll help you figure out which program fits you best.

Prep made personal.

Whether you want quick coaching in a particular GMAT subject area or a comprehensive study plan developed around your goals, we've got you covered. Our expert GMAT instructors can help you hit your top score.

CHECK OUT THESE REVIEWS FROM MANHATTAN PREP STUDENTS.

Contact us at 800-576-4628 or gmat@manhattanprep.com
for more information about your GMAT study options.